To the membership of the

AMERICAN ASSOCIATION
OF SUICIDOLOGY

On
the
Nature
of
Suicide

Edwin S. Shneidman, EDITOR

ON
THE
NATURE
OF
SUICIDE

Jossey-Bass Inc., Publishers
615 Montgomery Street · San Francisco · 1969

THE JOSSEY-BASS
BEHAVIORAL SCIENCE SERIES

General Editors

WILLIAM E. HENRY, *University of Chicago*

NEVITT SANFORD, *Wright Institute, Berkeley*

Contents

Contents

Authors

David Bakan, Ph.D., professor of psychology, York University, Toronto

Jacques Choron, Ph.D., D.S.Sc., former lecturer in philosophy, New School for Social Research; fellow, Center for Studies of Suicide Prevention, National Institute of Mental Health

Jack D. Douglas, Ph.D., associate professor of sociology, University of California, San Diego

Louis I. Dublin, Ph.D., vice-president and statistician (retired), Metropolitan Life Insurance Company

Leslie H. Farber, M.D., director of therapy, Austen Riggs Center, Stockbridge, Massachusetts

Authors

Paul Friedman, M.D., Ph.D., practicing psychoanalyst; attending staff, Mount Sinai Hospital, New York

Robert J. Havighurst, Ph.D., professor of education, Fordham University; professor emeritus of education and human development, University of Chicago

Sidney M. Jourard, Ph.D., professor of psychology, University of Florida

Lawrence Kubie, M.D., visiting professor of psychiatry, Jefferson Medical College of Philadelphia; clinical professor of psychiatry, University of Maryland School of Medicine; lecturer in psychiatry, The Johns Hopkins University School of Medicine

Karl Menninger, M.D., chairman of the board of trustees, The Menninger Foundation; senior consultant and acting director, Youth Mental Health Project, The Stone-Brandel Center, Chicago; university professor at large, University of Kansas

Edwin S. Shneidman, Ph.D., chief, Center for Studies of Suicide Prevention, National Institute of Mental Health; clinical professor of psychiatry (suicidology), George Washington University School of Medicine; lecturer in psychiatry, The Johns Hopkins University School of Medicine

Erwin Stengel, M.D., F.R.C.P., professor emeritus of psychiatry, University of Sheffield; vice-president, International Association for Suicide Prevention; past president, Royal Medico-Psychological Association

On
the
Nature
of
Suicide

Prologue

Fifty-eight Years

Edwin S. Shneidman

ᘓᘓᘓᘓᘓᘓᘓᘓᘓᘓᘓᘓᘓᘓᘓᘓᘓ

Gematria is defined as a mystical system for interpreting events and printed text (usually scriptural text) by means of giving special literal meanings to numbers and to combinations of numbers.[1] In this volume, the number for our special contemplation is *58*—the specific span of years between the 1910 psychoanalytic meetings on suicide in Vienna and the "reconvening" (at least, in spirit) of those meetings in 1968 at the first annual conference of the American Association of Suicidology in Chicago. The question is whether fifty-eight years is a long time or a short one. How is one to judge? Think of some of the mighty persons of history who died well before age fifty-eight. Think of your own chronological age and the meanings that fifty-eight years now have for you. Can you imagine your ever being as old as fifty-eight—or being fifty-eight again?

1

On the Nature of Suicide

How can one measure the length of a "fixed" time interval which is itself embedded in larger macrotemporal units in which passage through time seems to move at different speeds in different eras? In the twentieth century surely, fifty-eight years would, for many purposes, seem "long enough." Can one, extrapolating from the wondrous changes which have already occurred in this century in the fields of transportation, communication, and space exploration—to mention but a few—be led to expect that somewhat comparable changes have occurred in other areas, for example, in the conceptualizations relating to the nature of man, or the conceptualizations relating to self-destruction in man? The extent to which developments have occurred relating to theories of self-destruction in the fifty-eight-year interval between 1910 and 1968—and the explication of the nature of some of these changes—is the major focus of this volume.

To return to our initial temporal anchor point: 1910. The meetings in Vienna were highly unusual in a number of ways:

1. They were the only meetings held by the Vienna psychoanalytic group on the topic of suicide, a subject somehow generally eschewed by those pioneers of the mind.

2. They were meetings that were chaired not by Freud but by Adler, a point about which contemporary Adlerians are quite legitimately adamant.[2]

3. They were held on the temporal threshold of the splintering of the original psychoanalytic group—for within one short year several of the members (Adler, Jung, and Stekel included) had left Freud's main camp to set up new bivouacs of their own.

4. They were the occasion of the first enunciation, specifically by Wilhelm Stekel, of that perspicacious psychodynamic formulation that the yearning for the death of the self can only be the mirrored wish for the death of another—a

2

telling concept which has both enlightened and bedeviled almost all of the subsequent thinking about the psychodynamics of self-destruction.

5. They may very well have stimulated the development of Freud's own further thoughts on death and suicide. A brilliant historical exposition of the development of Freud's thinking on these topics appears in Litman's chapter, "Sigmund Freud on Suicide," in the recent *Essays in Self-Destruction.*[3]

6. They focused on the role of education—that is, the role of learning, pedagogy, and, in the most general way, the role of acculturation and environment—in suicide. Our heightened present-day concerns with campus hostility and street violence give us contemporary indication of the timeliness of the topics of learning and environment—and of the role of the school.

7. The 1910 meetings speak to us today, having addressed themselves to some of the ubiquitous and magnotemporal aspects of man, those omnipresent elements of man's make-up, especially the relation to his self-destructive drives and his often inimical roles in his own fate.

Among the several events relating to suicide prevention that were taking place in our own very recent past—specifically in 1967 when the initial plans for the first annual conference of the American Association of Suicidology were being formulated—was the timely appearance of Paul Friedman's edited version of the 1910 symposium.[4]

In the light of the fact that an especially stellar symposium was sought for that first program, could any idea have been better than to reconvene the spirit of the 1910 symposium with a contemporary group of distinguished scientists and clinicians, each of whom had written, with great impact, on the topics of suicide or death—and each one of whom was well alive in 1910, and—in fantasy at least—might, in one capacity or another, have attended that auspicious meeting in Vienna, fifty-eight years before? I think not.

Although no attempt was made to duplicate the points of view presented in the original symposium, an advertent effort was made to find someone to represent the interest comparable to David Ernst Oppenheim's original role, that is, someone representing the field of education and the school's place in both creating and preventing suicide. The participation of Robert Havighurst filled this need.

The general aim of the "reconvention" was to provide an opportunity for a dialogue among a select group of men of wisdom and experience. Accordingly, each person was asked to prepare a relatively brief paper representing some of his current views and beliefs about suicide. These presentations were supplemented at the symposium by a period of open interplay among the participants in order to develop further crosscurrents of discussion. The broad question to which each participant was asked to address himself was: "What now do we know about suicide since 1910?"

At the 1968 meeting there was also a symposium on "Self-Destruction and the Problem of the Will."[5] The topic of the will is much neglected in contemporary psychology and psychiatry. The earlier writings of Narcissus Ach and William James, to mention but two, on this topic now scarcely receive even passing interest in the psychological market, but the pivotal role of intention in self-destruction continues to be self-evident. Intending, of course, is an aspect of, if not synonymous with, willing. Recent books on these and related topics all provide a new permissiveness for a symposium on suicide and the will.[6] The papers by the four participants in that symposium are reproduced in this volume with the express feeling that they furnish important and relevant companion pieces to the papers and discussion by the seven elder statesmen of the suicide world.

4

Edwin S. Shneidman

Using Friedman's edited report of the 1910 proceedings as the general springboard for our further reflections, what can we say—from our perusal of the reports of the 1968 meetings, as well as from our knowledge of other current developments in this country—about what is *new* in the prevention of suicide? It is obvious that as recently as the past decade there have been a number of important developments in "suicidology," the scientific and humane study of human self-destruction. It seems to me that we presently stand at a major watershed in suicidological history; that there are a number of recent conceptual developments and major contemporary national changes and trends which are discernible and which merit special explication.

The conceptual developments, contemporary trends, and emerging patterns that come to mind constitute an impressive number of significant changes which reflect the changing nature of suicide. A listing will suffice to indicate something of their individual content and their total scope:

1. The current permissiveness to discuss and study suicide and death.

2. Suicide prevention and its elaborations, especially intervention and postvention.

3. Changes in the concepts of life and the concepts of death, especially to include notions like partial death, ghetto death, and subintentioned death.

4. Changes in the conceptualization of death, and in the format of the death certificate.

5. The varieties of intention in self-destruction.

6. The pivotal place of ambivalence in self-destruction.

7. The key role of the significant other in the suicidal dyad and the growing view of the suicidal crisis as a dyadic crisis.

8. The role of affective states other than hostility

in suicide, especially dependency, hopelessness, and helplessness.

9. A growing appreciation of the role of age (or time of life) in suicide.

10. The explication of suicidality along the dimensions of lethality and perturbation.

11. An appropriate emphasis on the delineation and dissemination of prodromal clues to suicide.

12. The implications and impacts of organ transplantation.

13. The impact of the massive secularization of death and the enormous spiritual and psychological problems thus created.

14. Some new looks at old masters, especially Freud and Durkheim.

15. Significant changes in the public practice of suicide prevention, especially in what services will be delivered.

16. Changes in the patterns of financial and community support for suicide prevention activities.

17. A growing emphasis on assessment, especially of the effectiveness of interventional efforts.

18. The recent appearance of suicide professionalism and the role of suicidology.

Now to discuss a half-dozen of these in detail.

1. *The current permissiveness (even the urgency) to discuss and study suicide and death.* We seem to be living at a time when death is in the air, reminding us of such previous times as that of the black plague, the barbarian invasions of Rome, the shattering earthquakes in Japan—all eras when the balance of life seemed to pause on a pointed fulcrum. Today, whatever a man's daily activities, he lives with some subliminal apperception of the possibility of global annihilation. The precedent of Nagasaki and Hiroshima beclouds every city and silo in the land. We and our potential enemies have long since

passed yesterday's capacity only to decimate—to kill one out of every ten. We (and they) now have the power to destroy cities completely and, in one blinding flash, simultaneously to expunge the future and to erase the past.

The existence of the bomb creates an intellectual permissiveness and affective urgency for the development of new attitudes toward the usual taboos surrounding the topics of death and suicide. My reading of the facts and horrors that Lifton has explicated in his haunting book *Death in Life*, has persuaded me that some psychological aftermath of the Hiroshima holocaust lives somewhere in the unconscious mind of almost every sensitive citizen.[7]

The comments of George Wald, Nobel laureate at Harvard, are relevant here:

> *I think that we are up against a generation that is by no means sure that it has a future. . . . That is the problem. Unless we can be surer than we now are that this generation has a future, nothing else matters. It's not enough to give it tender loving care . . . to buy it expensive education. These things don't mean anything unless this generation has a future, and we're not sure that it does.*[8]

The topic of death is timely. Its open discussion is part of the new unbooing of long-held taboos relating to sexuality, hostility, civility in behavior, and wanton destruction. (Along with the bomb, one must also consider the enormous impact of the pill, drugs, and the torturing war in which we are presently ambivalently entangled.)

One tangible manifestation of this decrease in taboo and the concomitant increase in interest is found in the upsurge of suicide prevention activities in this country in the past few years: (a) the establishment of the Center for Studies of Suicide Prevention at the National Institute of Mental Health (in 1966); (b) the increase in the number of suicide prevention centers in the United States, from only three as recently as 1958, to nine in 1964, to over one hundred in 1968 —an increase not totally unrelated to the first named development; (c) the initiation of a journal, the *Bulletin of Suicidology,* devoted to this topic (in 1967); (d) the founding of a national professional group, the American Association of Suicidology (in 1967)—to mention only a few of these recent impactful developments.

By way of constrast with the 1968 meeting on suicide, how benign the year 1910 now sounds: the days before effective airplanes (and effective aerial bombs), when the most powerful weapons were mounted on dreadnaughts one-tenth the tonnage of some present vessels. In many ways, that era seems closer to the time of the seemingly open suicidal emotions of Goethe's *Sorrows of Young Werther* than to our own. With all the ingenious life-extending inventions and marvels of science and technology, it yet seems that what man has done most effectively in the past fifty-eight years is to increase, at a rate that defies ordinary arithmetic, his dangerous capacities to slaughter.

2. *Re-evaluation of the role of affective states other than hostility in suicide.* Clearly, one of the most memorable pronouncements made at the 1910 symposium was Stekel's: to the effect that no one kills himself who has not wished for the death of another. Thereafter, the orthodox psychoanalytic formulation of the dynamics of suicide focused on hostility (seen as symbolic murder) as the single ubiquitous and universal affect in self-destruction. Suicide was viewed as the result of hateful rage misdirected toward a psychological aspect of interfused self-other. The psychological formulation became: suicide was hostility directed toward the introjected love object—what I have called murder in the 180th degree.

Litman's recent essay on Freud and suicide demonstrates that Freud's own thinking was more complex and catholic than the above formulation, although it is primarily only in the last ten to fifteen years, in part reflecting the writings of Litman himself, that the importance of considering a broader panoply of emotions has been clearly recognized. This enlarged scope includes especially the emotions of shame, guilt, and dependency, and perhaps most important of all, the affective states of hopelessness and helplessness. This is not to say that some individuals who commit suicide are clearly motivated by combinations of conscious or deeply unconscious hostility. Their suicide notes bristle with hatred, anger, and vengeance. But the fact is that most suicidal states—perhaps all—are characterized by deep currents of ambivalence; often ambivalence between the emotional states of hostility and affection (and almost always ambivalence between wanting to die and wanting to be rescued, where there may be a strong trend toward self-destruction and concomitant fantasies of intervention and rescue). It is not impossible to cut one's throat and to cry for help at the same time. It is also not impossible to hate and to love even in the suicidal act as this prototypical suicide note shows: "Dear Mary: I hate you. Love, George."

There is an obvious need for reformulations of the psychodynamics of self-destruction. Probably no one single formula will do. Clinically, we have seen that suicidal individuals who have high lethality are often characterized by the crushing combination of hopelessness and helplessness; that conjoint feeling that nothing can be done and that no one can do it. Not all despair grows out of anger, nor does it seem reasonable to believe that every suicide attempt is an attempt to expunge a hated homunculus in the breast. Several recent studies of suicide notes—still the best window into the cognitive and affective states accompanying the suicidal act—

indicate that the wide variety of deeply felt emotional states is apparently not amenable to reduction to any one single pervasive emotional state.

In 1910, the statement of an illuminating formulation was, scientifically and clinically, an exciting event; in 1968—after a period in which it seemed at times that statement had shaded into dogma—there was perhaps less focused excitement but, on the other hand, a more realistic awareness of the complexities of human self-destructive behaviors and of the various psychodynamic paths that may lead to them.

3. *A growing appreciation of the role of age or time of life in suicide.* Within the last twenty-five years, a number of studies have indicated that there are significantly different attitudes toward death at different ages—in childhood, adolescence, adulthood, and old age, for example. Analyses of suicide notes from young adults, middle-aged persons, and old adults have yielded corroborative evidence. In short, there is a growing appreciation of the significant role of age or time of life in suicide. In this sense, age is not tied exclusively to chronological age, but refers more meaningfully to "psychological age" or "philosophical age" or age-in-relation-to-one's-own-death. Age refers to the life-phase ages of the individual and what he does at each stage in his life. (In the Foreword to the second edition of his *Childhood and Society*,[9] Erikson reflects that his students counseled him against making any extensive revisions, conveying the feeling that "tampering with an itinerary written in younger years was not one of an older man's prerogatives.") One's attitudes about death, including especially one's attitude about his own suicide, would seem to be different at different phases of one's life. Litman's essay on Freud and my own essay on Melville show us the development of an individual's orientations toward his own annihilation over the broad range of his own psychological history. To the over-simple inquiry: "What was Freud's (or Melville's) think-

ing about death?" one can respond with the counterquestion: "To what stage of his life are you referring?" Attitudes toward death, perhaps much more than attitudes toward other important topics, are age-related.[10]

One important implication of this insight is that it is not likely that one all-encompassing psychology of suicide will be forthcoming. What is more likely is that we shall have psychologies of self-destruction, each relating most relevantly to a specific stage in life. These might be tied to such conceptualizations as Shakespeare's ages of man, Erikson's psychosocial stages in the human life cycle, Heard's stages of man, Sullivan's developmental epochs, Charlotte Buhler's stages in the human course of life, Schachtel's periods in the human metamorphosis, Jung's two main stages of man's life, or some newly developed concept of death orientation in man.

It may well be that explanations of self-destruction—even when they take account of multiple causation and even when they include views from several disciplines—will need to be multiple in their nature, resonating to the total range of conceivable ages-in-relation-to-death. Weisman and Hackett's concept of "an appropriate death" captures the flavor of this notion. They ask:

> *What makes one death appropriate and another death tragic? It is strange that, while medicine presides daily over unnumbered deaths and psychiatrists study the psychopathology of death in its protean forms, death has so universally been regarded as a dark symbol beyond investigation. Psychiatrists do not hesitate to study various types of suicide, but the reverse of a suicidal situation, one in which the prospect of appropriate resolution in death far outweighs the fear of dissolution by dying, is rarely mentioned.*
>
> *Part of an answer to this is to be found in the aversion among doctors to confront themselves with the fact of their own death and to wonder if death can ever be*

appropriate for them. Despair wears many masks; a hard shell of materialism may cover a tenderness that shuns exposure. The dedication to forestall death is an indication that the medical profession believes that death is never appropriate.

A death that is appropriate for one person may be quite out of character for another. For most people martyrdom holds little appeal as an appropriate death, nor do we tend to glorify death. . . .

The concept of an appropriate death is one so alien to most people that it is difficult to obtain an accurate appraisal of the circumstances in which any individual patient would be prepared to die. Although he faces the fact that living comes to an end, he finds it easier to imagine the conditions under which he might commit suicide. What responses would most people make if they were asked to write their own eulogies? Would it be easier to write a proposed suicide note than an obituary? Under what circumstances, for example, would the reader be willing to die? It is as difficult to propose an appropriate personal death, such as dying for a cause; or of interpersonal death, such as reunion with a lost love; or even of intrapersonal death, such as resurrection, does not adequately define an appropriate death. All three personal dimensions are necessary if this concept is to have meaning.

Our hypothesis is that, whatever its content, an appropriate death must satisfy four principal requirements: (1) conflict is reduced; (2) compatibility with the ego ideal is achieved; (3) continuity of important relationships is preserved or restored; (4) consummation of a wish is brought about. This does not mean, of course, that under the usual circumstances of dying it is possible to attain a death that is as wholly acceptable as it was to the predilection patients. Nevertheless, planning and implementing psychotherapeutic interventions in other patients who are certain to die may be facilitated if these criteria are used as guides, together with the psychodynamic formulation of the patient's private concerns.[11]

Earlier, I referred to the special use of suicide notes written by victims of different ages. In 1957, Norman Farberow and I analyzed 619 suicide notes of 489 men (ages twenty to ninety-six) and 130 women (ages twenty to seventy-eight). The subjects were divided into three age groups: twenty to thirty-nine, forty to fifty-nine, and sixty and over. All the notes were analyzed in terms of Menninger's tripartite approach: the wish to kill, the wish to be killed, and the wish to die. The analysis indicated that, in general, for both sexes, the intensity of the wish to kill and the wish to be killed decreased with advancing age, while the intensity of the wish to die increased with age. The most significant single result was the finding that the psychodynamics of suicide, at least as indicated by an analysis of the suicide notes with this method of approach, were different for each of the three age groupings.[12]

In an attempt to reflect the impact of psychological age on suicide, one might think of three types of suicide notes and, by extension, three types of suicidal acts as follows:

Egotic suicides are those in which the self-imposed death may be identified primarily with an *intrapsychic* process —a debate, disputation, or dialogue within the mind. In contrast, the impact of the immediate environment, the presence of friends or loved ones, the existence, "out there," of group ties or sanctions become secondary and distant perceptual "ground" as compared with the urgency of internal psychic debate. The dialogue is within the personality; it is a conflict among aspects of the self. Such deaths can be seen as "egocide" or ego destruction; they are annihilations of the self or the personality. At the time of the self-destruction, the individual is primarily "self-contained" and responds to the voices (not in the sense of hallucinatory voices) within him. Thus one sees extremely narrowed focus of attention, self-denigrating depression, and other situations where suicide occurs seemingly without regard for loved ones and significant others.

Such individuals are often viewed by professionals as delusional, although sometimes the agitated obsessional quality is what is seen most clearly. They are self-contained, in the sense that the person's torment is "within the head" as in the anguish of a Virginia Woolf, or the torment of an Ellen West. Many of the "crazy" (that is, psychotic, gifted, excessively neurotic, "special," private, inwardly convoluted, highly symbolic) suicides are of this nature. These suicides can be conceptualized in a number of special ways, such as nihilistic, oceanic, reunion, Harlequin, magical, and so on.

Egotic suicides are thus primarily psychological in their nature. Notes left by this kind of suicidal person contain explanations of these special inner states. They are filled with symbolism and metaphor and sometimes poetry (although rarely poetry of superior quality). These suicide notes are special windows not so much into the ideation or affect of the anguished person as they are private views of idiosyncratic existential struggles and inner unresolved philosophic disputations. Usually, suicide notes of this type are private notes addressed to the self; when they are addressed to specific persons they are then meant as didactic explanations of the victim's inner world of choice.

Individuals who commit this type of suicide have in common a phenomenon which can be called "boggling." The person boggles (that is, refuses to go on because of doubt, fear, scruple, confusion, pain, and so on). It is as though he says to himself, "So far and absolutely no further." Colloquially translated, it comes out as, "I've had it." He has taken as many of the world's assaults as he cares to take; his limits or tolerance for continuing his bargain with life have been reached and he is now abrogating that relationship.

Dyadic suicides are those in which the death relates

primarily to the deep unfulfilled needs and wishes pertaining to the significant partner in the victim's life. These suicides are primarily dyadic and thus *social* and relational in their nature. Although suicide is always the act of a single person and, in this sense, stems from within one mind, the dyadic suicide is essentially an interpersonal event. In these cases, the cries refer to the frustration (of love and the search for love), hate, anger, disappointment, shame, guilt, rage, impotence, and rejection in relation to the other *him* or *her*—either the real him or her or a symbolic (or even fantasied or fictional) person. The key to the act lies in the unfulfilled need: "If only he (or she) would . . ." Suicide notes, usually prefaced by the word, "Dear," are typically addressed to a specific person, an ambivalently loved one. Most suicides are dyadic; they are primarily transactional in nature. The victim's best eggs are in the other person's flawed basket. He (and his figurative eggs) are crushed. The dyadic suicidal act may reflect the victim's penance, bravado, revenge, plea, histrionics, self-punishment, gift of life, withdrawal, fealty, disaffiliation, or whatever—but its arena is primarily interpersonal and its understanding (and thus its meaning) cannot occur outside the dyadic relationship.

Ageneratic suicides are those in which the self-inflicted deaths relate primarily to the individual's falling out of his sense of a procession of generations. He has lost (or abrogated) his feeling of membership in the inexorable march of generations and, in this sense, his membership in the human race itself. Most individuals sense a belonging to a whole line of generations; fathers and grandfathers and great-grandfathers before him, and children and grandchildren and great-grandchildren after him. An ageneratic suicide has lost this sense of temporal identification. He is psychologically an old man.

Erikson has used the term *generativity* to represent the concern of one generation for the next—"the interest for

15

establishing and guiding the next generation"—in which the general idea is one of transgenerational relationships. He further points out that where this sense of generativity is absent in the adult individual, there is often "a pervading sense of individual stagnation and interpersonal impoverishment." In most of the important interpersonal adult exchanges, one does not ordinarily expect direct or reciprocal reward or repayment; rather, as in parenthood, what one desires is that the next generation do at least as much for their next generation as he has done. The person who falls out of his society or out of his lineage is a person who has lost investment in his own "post-self"—that which continues after his death. This kind of suicide grows out of alienation, disengagement, familial ennui, aridity, and emptiness of the individaul as he stands in the family of man. The sense of belonging to the stream of generations is illustrated in a published letter (dated October, 1967) by Arnold Toynbee in which he said, "I am now an old man and most of my treasure is therefore in future generations. This is why I care so much." The ageneratic suicide has lost this sense of treasure and that is why he cares so little.

This sense of belongingness and place in the scheme of things, especially in the march of generations, is not only an aspect of middle and old age, but it is the comfort and characteristic of psychological maturity at whatever age. To have no sense of serial belongingness or to be, in Melville's term, an "isolato" is truly a lonely and comfortless position. In that perspective, one may have very little to live for. This kind of hermit is estranged not only from his contemporaries, but much more importantly, he is alienated from his forebears and his descendants; from his own inheritance and his own bequests. He is without a sense of the majestic flow of the generations—he is ageneratic. Ageneratic suicides are primarily sociological in nature, relating as they do to familial, cultural, national, or group ties. Suicide notes of this type are often (although not always) addressed "To whom it may concern," "To the police," or not addressed at all. They seem to be muted voices in a macrotemporal void.

Not only are suicidal phenomena different events at different stages of life, but suicidal acts may have different relationships to any one stage of life. At least three can be outlined: intratemporal suicide, that is, one which occurs within a phase of life and reflects the psychological issues and conflicts characteristic of that time of life; intertemporal suicide, that is, one which occurs between phases of a life and thereby reflects the problems of turning from one phase to another or the special problems which exist in the interstices or vacuums when one is psychologically beyond one phase but has not quite reached or accepted the next; and extratemporal suicide, that is, one which occurs independent of the phase of life, especially in individuals who are out of phase with their own lives, who have precociously savored experiences too early or, conversely, have not grown up emotionally and are innocent beyond their years. Extratemporal suicides, which may occur during any phase of life, also include those acts which are essentially resonating panic reactions to some substantive disturbance, but which, at the moment of self-destruction (like acute stage fright) are taken up entirely with the reverberating anxiety so that the precipitating reasons are almost totally obscured.

All this is to suggest that in 1968, as contrasted with 1910, suicidologists had a much more keen appreciation of the developmental nature of man's mental life. One major implication of this view is that the suicidal acts of sixteen-, thirty-six-, and seventy-six-year-old individuals can be understood only by taking into account their sex (and sexual orientations), socioeconomic status, minority affiliations and frustrations, physiological state (including drugs and alcohol), and their age.

4. *Changes in the conceptualizations of death.* From the point of view of the history of ideas, perhaps the most important impact of the 1910 symposium was its implicit presentation of the concept of the unconscious psychodynamics of death. The implication is clearly there: that the kinds of death could no longer be dichotomized into what I shall call felonious and adventitious. (Felonious deaths were of two types: the crime of homicide and suicide, which was called a *felo de se,* implying that the victim and culprit were combined in the same person. Adventitious deaths were also of two types: natural and accidental, implying that death was due to "chance" or "nature" or was "an act of God" and that there was no culpability. These four *modes* of death—natural, accident, suicide, and homicide (what I have called the *NASH* classification of modes of death)—are to be distinguished from the more than one hundred *causes* of death which can often be identified with one or more modes of death (for example, asphyxiation due to drowning or overdose of barbiturates could, in these traditional terms, be accidental, suicidal, or homicidal).

The 1910 symposium trichotomized death by opening the middle ground between intentioned deaths and unintentioned deaths to insert the role of the unconscious in death —what I have called subintentioned death.[13] This larger tripartite view of death is implied throughout the 1910 symposium in the remarks of each contributor with the understandable exception of those of the pedagogue, Ernst Oppenheim.

In 1968, thanks especially to such post-1910 psychoanalytic thinkers in this country as Zilboorg, Menninger, Litman, and others, we are keenly aware of the subtle, covert,

Edwin S. Shneidman

latent, partial, and unconscious roles of the individual in effecting or, more often, in hastening his own demise. Clinically, we know through our psychological autopsies of the intensively effective psychological overlay in many so-called natural, accidental, suicidal, and homicidal deaths. (In these subintentioned deaths one finds critical premortem behaviors such as excessive risk taking, imprudence, changes in life-style, disregard of life-extending medical regimen, neglect of self, misuse of drugs and alcohol, and so on). The psychosomatics of death is now a rather generally accepted concept.

Further: although not explicitly discussed in the 1968 symposium, what was clearly implied—at least in my hearing of it—was a considerable extension of this basic concept of the unconscious elements in human death. These new forays would include such concepts as partial deaths, ghetto deaths, subintentioned deaths, "student suicidalism,"[14] non-adventitious "accidents" (subcidents), and the even broader arena of psychologically laden inimical and reductive behaviors—subintentioned partial deaths—such as certain patterns of psychosis, addiction, alcoholism, prostitution, delinquency, incivility, underachievement, and ennui. There are numerous ways of committing partial suicide and permitting partial death, all truncations of the spirit. A comprehensive monograph on the nature of suicide—yet to be written—would, perforce, have to include these topics and make them central.

5. *Suicide prevention and its current elaborations, especially suicide intervention and postvention.* Traditionally, in public health circles, one speaks of primary, secondary, and tertiary *pre*vention. I believe that it would be more meaningful—using the same Latin root (*venire,* to come)—to divide the term along its temporal dimension and to speak of prevention, intervention, and postvention, referring to the helpful activities which occur before, during and after a stressful or dangerous situation.

19

On the Nature of Suicide

Prevention: The suicide prevention centers of this country can, by and large, be more accurately described as suicide interventional centers, dealing, as they do, with crises already in process. Their main function is to mollify or diminish the intensity of the already-present occurrence by employing whatever interventional techniques are available and appropriate.

On the other hand, prevention of suicide—that is, focusing efforts on seeing that the inimical event does not occur in the first place— involves one, willy-nilly, in the broad (and fuzzy) topics of prevention of mental health dysfunctions and maladies in general. Such a discussion involves such major topical areas as eugenics, freedom from congenital defects, optimal parent-child relations, benign social and cultural environment—all those forces that relate to the later occurrence of such sociopsychological blights as delinquency, alcoholism, addiction, schizophrenia, and suicide.

On a practical level, prevention of suicide involves the identification of high-risk groups (and individuals within them); the ready availability of responsive services; the dissemination of information, particularly about prodromal clues; the lowering of taboos so that citizens can more easily ask for help; the sensitization of professionals and ordinary citizens to the recognition of potential suicide; and so on.

Intervention: In the past few years, there has been a special focus and an attendant spurt of interest in the interventional and postventional aspects of suicide. Intervention in suicide—a vast area developed almost entirely in the last fifteen years—incorporates relatively new techniques for crisis intervention (itself a rather recent concept) involving a number of procedures and techniques which have been evolved in the last decade. These include: (a) the recognition of the dyadic nature of suicidal crises and the concomitant recognition of the necessity of involving the significant other in the

20

helping process; (b) an approach to the problem from the point of view of crisis theory—concepts developed largely by Lindemann and Caplan—with the specific and general role of diminishing the individual's level of perturbation, and in the case of suicidal individuals of mollifying the level of the individual's lethality (that is, the probability of his killing himself); (c) the increased referral to agencies and resources within the community, including liaison with aspects of the community such as the police, board of education, and social agencies; and special affiliations with the community mental health centers—to mention a few; and (d) the development of a stance involving much more activity on the part of clinical suicidologists. Their fealty must be to the goal of keeping a lethal person alive. They must, on occasion, appropriately put aside such clearly secondary issues as the possibility of exacerbating the person's dependency or reinforcing his negative behavior. For an individual who is in an acute lethality state, the appropriate responses seem to be to involve others and to do almost anything (even catering to his infantile idiosyncrasies) which will successfully see him through the lethal crisis. Of course, crises of lower lethality (with different degrees of perturbation) may require different stratagems and techniques for appropriate response.

Postvention: I have proposed the term *postvention* to label activities which occur after a suicidal event. These postventive efforts can be of two types: (a) working with an individual after he has made a suicide attempt—with the obvious goals of decreasing the probability of any subsequent attempt and of mollifying the consequences of the recent attempt; and (b) working with the survivor-victims of a committed suicide to help them with their anguish, guilt, anger, shame, and perplexity.

A few years ago, Erich Lindemann wrote an article entitled "Preventative Intervention in the Case of a Five-

On the Nature of Suicide

Year-Old Whose Father Committed Suicide." I submit that Lindemann might have used the word *postvention* had it been available to him.

Postvention aims primarily at mollifying the psychological sequelae of a suicidal death in the survivor-victim. It may be said that, in our culture, there are only two kinds of mourning and grief patterns: those which accrue to an ordinary death from heart or cancer or accident or whatever, and, on the other hand, those which relate to the stigmatizing death of a loved one by suicide. The person who commits suicide puts his psychological skeleton in the survivor's emotional closet—he sentences the survivor to a complex of negative feelings and, most importantly, to obsessing about the reasons for the suicide death.

A benign community ought routinely to provide immediate postventive mental health care for the survivor-victims of suicidal deaths. Postvention is prevention for the next decade and for the next generation. It may be said that of the three approaches to mental health—prevention, intervention, and postvention—that, in relation to suicide, postvention contributes to the largest aspect of the total problem. Consider: there may be about 50,000 suicidal deaths in the United States each year. Further, it is rather accurately documented that there are about eight suicide attempts for each case of committed suicide, and still further and perhaps most importantly, that for each committed suicide there are an estimated half-dozen survivor-victims whose lives are thereafter benighted by that event. We are now talking about 750,000 persons each year who are intimately affected by suicidal behavior. A comprehensive local or national program in suicidology must include these three interrelated components of prevention, intervention, and postvention. These notions were scarcely apperceived in 1910.

6. *A focus on the dyadic nature of suicide and*

22

death. I regret not having thought to invite Arnold Toynbee to the 1968 Suicidology symposium, even though I have no reason at all to believe that he would have accepted an invitation. His recent edited book on death—*Man's Concern with Death*—qualified him completely as an active thanatologist. It is about his personal and moving epilogue to that book that I wish to make my concluding remarks in this preface.

With some passionate emphasis, Toynbee states the point that death is essentially a dyadic event.

> *The spectacle of insanity and senility has always appalled me more than witnessing or the hearing of a physical death. But there are two sides to this situation; there is the victim's side, as well as the spectator's; and what is harrowing for the spectator may be alleviating for the victim. . . . This two-sidedness of death is a fundamental feature of death—not only of the premature death of the spirit, but of death at any age and in any form. There are always two parties to a death; the person who dies and the survivors who are bereaved. . . .*
>
> *If one truly love a fellow human being, one ought to wish that as little as possible of the pain of his or her death shall be suffered by him or by her, and that as much of it as possible shall be borne by oneself. One ought to wish this, and one can, perhaps, succeed in willing it with one's mind. But can one genuinely desire it in one's heart? Can one genuinely long to be the survivor at the coming time when death will terminate a companionship without which one's own life would be a burden, not a boon? Is it possible for love to raise human nature to his height of unselfishness? I cannot answer this question for anyone except myself, and, in my own case, before the time comes, I can only guess what my reaction is likely to be. I have already avowed a boastful guess that I shall be able to meet my own death with equanimity. I have now to avow another guess that puts me to shame. I guess that if, one day, I am told by my doctor that I am*

going to die before my wife, I shall receive the news not only with equanimity but with relief. This relief, if I do feel it, will be involuntary. I shall be ashamed of myself for feeling it, and my relief will, no doubt, be tempered by concern and sorrow for my wife's future after I have been taken from her. All the same, I do guess that, if I am informed that I am going to die before her, a shameful sense of relief will be one element in my reaction.

My own conclusion is evident. My answer to Saint Paul's question "O death, where is thy sting?" is Saint Paul's own answer: "The sting of death is sin." The sin that I mean is the sin of selfishly failing to wish to survive the death of someone with whose life my own life is bound up. This is selfish because the sting of death is less sharp for the person who dies than it is for the bereaved survivor.

This is, as I see it, the capital fact about the relation between living and dying. There are two parties to the suffering that death inflicts; and, in the apportionment of this suffering, the survivor takes the brunt.[15]

I have some empirical data relevant to Toynbee's assertions. Two items from the questionnaire used in the Psychology of Death course (which I taught at Harvard in Spring, 1969) are related to Toynbee's topic. One question was, "If and when you are married, would you prefer to outlive your spouse or would you prefer your spouse to outlive you? Discuss your reasons."

The data from this research on 90 Harvard men and 30 Radcliffe women indicate that more women than men want to die together with their spouses or first, before their spouses; and that more men than women want to die second, after their spouses. This difference is significant at the .01 level, that is, this finding could hardly occur by chance. It was clear that the modal male response was to prefer to die second; the modal female response was to prefer to die first. Toynbee's pronouncements, at the age of eighty, seem consistent with the younger Harvard people of the same sex. An appropriate question would be to ask what Mrs. Toynbee would have written on this same topic.

The data on the reasons given for the timing preference show that more women than men gave as a reason for their timing choice wanting to avoid loneliness or grief; that more men than women gave as their reason wanting to spare their spouses the anguish of grief or feeling better able to cope with life alone than their spouses. The eighteen-to-twenty-two-year-old Harvard male is, at least in his fantasy, protective of his spouse. This finding was also significant at the .01 level. In summary: the typical male response was to choose to die after his wife, giving as his reason that a widower can do better than can a widow; the typical female response was to choose to die first, giving as her reason the desire to avoid the loneliness of widowhood.

Another item in the questionnaire read: "Rank the following statements about the consequences of your own death from 1 to 7, where 1 indicates the least distasteful and 7 the most distasteful." Table 1 presents the mean, mode, and rank order of the seven items for males and females. What is to be noted is although items 1, 2, 3, and 5 were ranked identically for the two sexes, the item "I could no longer care for my dependents" is ranked as third most distasteful by the males (after "I could no longer have any experiences" and "My death would cause grief to my relatives and friends") and was ranked as fifth most distasteful by the females. This result is consistent with the previous item and Toynbee's assertion about males in relation to death in a dyadic relationship.

In terms of Toynbee's notion of there being two parties to death and the relative suffering it inflicts on the person who dies and on the survivor—and his idea that "the sting of death is less sharp for the person who dies than it is

25

for the bereaved"—Harvard undergraduate males are far more sympathetic to Toynbee's attitude toward death than are the Radcliffe females. Males, far more than females, expressed the wish to spare their spouses the difficulty, anguish, and grief of loss, and bereavement, and so by Toynbee's criteria would seem more truly to love their potential spouses. Perhaps this is a reflection of a more mature set of males and of their potential protective masculine role in the marriage.

In focusing on the importance of the dyadic relationship in death, Toynbee renders a great conceptual service to suicidology, for in suicide—typically an intensely dyadic event—and specifically in suicide prevention, the role of the significant other in the total responding and rescuing process is now understood to be of paramount importance. Indeed, much of what is new in suicide intervention focuses around the active use of the dyadic partner: the spouse, lover, parent, child, or whoever.

Although it is difficult to take a stance counter to Toynbee's sentimental and seemingly persuasive position, nevertheless I believe that, in emphasizing the dyadic nature of death, Toynbee seems to have overlooked the key distinction—a distinction made by Bridgman and, in a very different context, by Laing—between the individual as he experiences himself and the individual as he is experienced by others.[16] Death—being dead—is not an experienceable experience at all. If one can experience anything at all he is, of course, not dead. The living experience of fearing or anticipating or thinking about one's death, like the experience of a period that one believes to be his own dying, cannot be shared in that it happens only in the mind of the experiencer. Of the total sum of dyadic pain, most is certainly borne by the survivor in cases of sudden deaths; but in protracted dying, the present pain and the anguish involved in the lugubrious anticipation of being dead may well be sharper for the dying person than the

Table 1

RANKING OF CONSEQUENCES OF DEATH

	MALE			FEMALE		
	Mean	Mode	Order	Mean	Mode	Order
I could no longer have any experiences.	4.8	7	1	5.7	7	1
I am uncertain as to what might happen to my body after death.	2.8	1	7	2.0	1	7
I am uncertain as to what might happen to me if there is a life after death.	3.7	2	6	2.5	2	6
I could no longer care for my dependents.	4.5	5	3	4.2	5	5
My death would cause grief to my relatives and friends.	4.6	5	2	4.8	4	2
All my plans and projects would come to an end.	4.2	4	4	4.4	6	3
The process of dying might be painful.	4.1	4	5	4.3	3	4

pain suffered then and after by the survivor. The algebra of death's suffering is a complicated equation.

For all his wisdom, Toynbee is indulging unduly in what I would call the romanticization of death. In my view, the larger need is to deromanticize death and suicide.

Certainly one of the most remarkable characteristics of man's psychological life is the undiluted and enduring love-affair that each of us has with his own consciousness. Trapped, as he is, within his own mind, man nurtures his conscious awareness, accepts it as the criterion for mediating reality, and entertains a faithful lifelong dialogue with it— even (or especially) when he "loses his mind" or "takes leave of his senses." Often, man communicates with his mind as though it were a separate "other," whereas it is really himself with whom he is constantly in communication. Indeed, the self-other to whom he talks is what, in large part, he defines himself to be. In light of all this, the great threat of death is that, like a cruel stepmother shouting at the excited children near the end of a full day's adventure, it orders a stop to this fascinating conversation-within-the-self. Death peremptorily decrees an abrupt, unwelcome, and final adjournment and dissolution of what Henry Murray has called "the congress of the mind." Death—being dead—is total cessation, personal naughtment, individual annihilation. It is the enemy and, ordinarily, one should not defect to it, embrace it, rationalize its supposed noble qualities, or even romanticize it as part of dyadic love.

One main difficulty with death is that, within himself each man is noble—that is, indestructible and all-surviving. One can, as Eldridge Cleaver has in his own naked way, put his "soul on ice," or, at the other thermal extreme, one can bank the fires of his own passions (as does Narcissus in Hesse's *Narcissus and Goldmund*), but, for a number of conscious or unconscious reasons, it is next to impossible to defect from one's loyalty to his own consciousness. Being conscious is all one has; that is what life is.

Life—being conscious of oneself—has two aspects: its duration (its length or shortness) and its scope (its richness or aridity). All too often nowadays we see individuals shorten the number of days of their lives and, equally tragic, we see them truncate, narrow, and demean the scope or breadth or richness of their lives. In 1968, as in 1910, clinical and research suicidologists have this extension of life's length and broadening of life's scope as the challenging dimensions of their legitimate concern.

References

[1] *Gematria* is defined in *Webster's New International Dictionary* but does not appear in the less complete *Webster's Collegiate Dictionary*. A recent fictional accounting of gematria appears in Chaim Potok's popular novel, *The Chosen* (New York: Simon and Schuster, 1967).

[2] See Hans Ansbacher, "Adler and the 1910 Symposium on Suicide: A Special Review," *Journal of Individual Psychology, 24,* November, 1968, 181–191, which details the historical circumstances surrounding the 1910 symposium on suicide.

[3] Robert E. Litman, "Sigmund Freud on Suicide." In Edwin S. Shneidman (Ed.), *Essays in Self-Destruction* (New York: Science House, 1967).

[4] Paul Friedman (Ed.), *On Suicide* (New York: International Universities Press, 1967).

[5] The first annual conference of the American Association of Suicidology at which these two symposia were presented—specifically on March 20, 1968, at the Conrad Hilton Hotel in Chicago, Illinois—was supported by a grant from the National Institute of Mental Health to William E. Henry, Committee on Human Relations, University of Chicago. We are all indebted to Henry in a number of ways: as project director of the conference

grant, as chairman of the symposium on "Self-Destruction and the Problem of the Will," and as general editor of Jossey-Bass, Inc., for the publication of these proceedings.

[6] David Bakan, *Disease, Pain, and Sacrifice* (Chicago: University of Chicago Press, 1968); Jack Douglas, *The Social Meanings of Suicide* (Princeton, N.J.: Princeton University Press, 1967); Leslie Farber, *The Ways of the Will* (New York: Basic Books, 1966); Sidney Jourard, *Disclosing Man to Himself* (Princeton, N.J.: Van Nostrand, 1968).

[7] Robert J. Lifton, *Death in Life: Survivors of Hiroshima* (New York: Random House, 1968).

[8] George Wald, quoted in *The New Yorker,* March 22, 1969.

[9] Erik H. Erikson, *Childhood and Society,* Revised edition (New York: Norton, 1964).

[10] Litman, *op. cit.;* Edwin S. Shneidman, "The Deaths of Herman Melville." In Howard P. Vincent (Ed.), *Melville and Hawthorne in the Berkshires* (Kent, Ohio: Kent State University Press, 1967).

[11] Avery D. Weisman and Thomas P. Hackett, "Predilection to Death: Death and Dying as a Psychiatric Problem," *Psychosomatic Medicine, 23,* 1961, 232–256.

[12] Edwin S. Shneidman and Norman L. Farberow, *Clues to Suicide* (New York: McGraw-Hill, 1957).

[13] Edwin S. Shneidman, "Orientations toward Death." In Robert W. White (Ed.), *The Study of Lives* (New York: Atherton, 1963).

[14] Lewis S. Feuer, *The Conflict of Generations: The Character and Significance of Student Movements* (New York: Basic Books, 1969).

[15] Arnold Toynbee (Ed.), *Man's Concern with Death* (London: Hodder and Stoughton, 1968).

[16] Percy W. Bridgman, *The Way Things Are* (Cambridge: Harvard University Press, 1959); R. D. Laing, *The Politics of Experience* (New York: Pantheon, 1967).

ONE

A SYMPOSIUM
ON SUICIDE

1

Jacques Choron

Mortality
and Death

Inasmuch as my connection with suicidology is an
outgrowth of my interest in the philosophical reflection about
mortality[1] as well as in the diversity of attitudes toward death,[2]
it is quite natural that I should focus my presentation on the
relationship between suicide and notions of death. This is all
the more appropriate inasmuch as attention to this relationship
is one of the newest developments in the study of suicidal
phenomena.

33

On the Nature of Suicide

It is somewhat surprising that, although suicide is an act in which death appears as a means as well as an end, the possible bearing on self-destructive behavior of a suicidal person's attitudes toward death and his notions about it has not been given serious consideration until quite recently. It is true that passing references have been made about the influence of the belief of an afterlife on suicidal acts, but this is a far cry from Wahl's statement[3] that "one cannot truly understand the deeper dynamics of suicide until he comprehends its relationship to death and the unconscious significance and meaning death has for us." Similarly, Hendin[4] stated that "the suicidal patient's attitudes toward death, dying and afterlife must be known in order to understand his motivations," and he described some of the psychodynamic patterns seen in suicidal patients in connection with different fantasies which they had about death.

For my part, I have suggested in a recent paper,[5] based in part on my work at the Los Angeles Suicide Prevention Center, that not only the unconscious meanings but also the consciously held convictions concerning death have to be explored and that it may be important that the latter are not necessarily identical with the fantasies exhibited by a person after he became suicidal. I further suggested that the notions of death held by any person may be classified as either potentially suicide-promoting or suicide-inhibiting. In particular, I have called attention to the probability that the notion of death as a kind of sleep is in itself suicide-promoting. Obviously, the distinction between suicide-promoting and suicide-inhibiting notions of death does not assume that only pleasant or innocuous representations of death are suicide-promoting. The matter is, of course, much more complicated. Thus, for a guilt-ridden person (in Menninger's terms, one dominated by the "wish to be killed"),[6] the notion of eternal punishment in

34

hell may be suicide-promoting, whereas for other people it usually serves as a suicide-inhibitor.

Finally, I have proposed that the therapist ought to attempt to discredit suicide-promoting notions and that, in general, an inquiry into the patient's notions and attitudes toward death should be made as a matter of routine, since such a procedure may have diagnostic as well as therapeutic values.

As to the possibility of manipulating the notions of death, we have to remember the frequent inconsistency in people's attitudes and views of death. Lester[7] has recently shown that some individuals may agree with both the following statements: "Death comes to comfort us" and "Death is the last and worst insult to man." We may add that to assume that a negative attitude to life automatically entails a positive attitude toward death is also an oversimplification. We have only to recall St. Augustine's revealing self-observation in his *Confessions: "Tedium vitae erat in me tremendum et moriendi metus"*—"There was in me a great weariness with life and also a great fear of dying." It is equally mistaken to assume that a positive attitude toward death and dying must necessarily shape the suicidal person's notions of death, since most notions of death have been formed, and sometimes have become deeply ingrained, long before any suicidal intent may make its appearance.

Another aspect of the relationship between death and suicide has also recently come under scrutiny on the part of some suicidologists, namely, the one implied by the concept of the death "instinct." I am referring here in particular to Litman's recent essay, "Sigmund Freud on Suicide,"[8] and to Tabachnick and Klugman's paper, "Suicide Research and the Death Instinct."[9]

It is interesting that only ten years after Freud had

stated in the 1910 Symposium on Suicide of the Vienna Psychoanalytical Society how little was actually known about suicidal phenomena, especially "how it becomes possible for the extraordinarily powerful life instinct to be overcome,"[10] he made his famous excursion into metapsychology (or, rather metaphysics) by postulating the existence of an equally powerful death drive (*Todestrieb*). By doing so he not only gave an answer to the above question, but also provided a challenging theory of suicide. I have reviewed in another place[11] the arguments for and against this controversial theory and want to limit myself now to a review of the antecedents of the term and concept of the death drive. As early as the first century A.D. Seneca used the expression *libido moriendi,* which is as close to the meaning of *Todestrieb* as its English rendering ("death instinct") is misleading. I do not know whether Freud ever objected to this mistranslation. In any case the term *l'instinct de la mort* has been used around the turn of the century by Metchnikoff[12] when he conjectured a desire for death which would appear in anyone who has reached the limit of man's natural life-span. This is obviously quite different from a basic death drive assumed by Freud. As for the term *Todestrieb,* Stekel had used it already by 1908, and it can be found much earlier in German literature and philosophy, notably in Hegel.

As far as the concept of the death drive in the Freudian meaning of the term is concerned, the real precursor appears to be Leonardo da Vinci, who speaks of "the hope and desire of going back to primal chaos, like that of the moth to the light . . . this longing which in its quintessence is the spirit of the elements . . . and inherent in Nature."[13] Of particular interest in this connection is Freud's "controversy" with Schopenhauer. Freud denies that he has "unwittingly steered his course into the harbor of Schopenhauer's philosophy, for whom death is the true result, and to that extent the purpose of life," and proceeds to enumerate what he assumes to be the important differences between their respective positions. "We do not assert that death is the only aim of life; we do not overlook the presence of life by the side of death. We recognize two fundamental drives and ascribe to each of them its own aim."[14] Although Freud is correct in saying that Schopenhauer considered death the only aim of life, it is not at all certain that he is right in respect to the other differences. It is hard to see how Schopenhauer, for whom the universal Will manifests itself in the organic realm as the "will to live," can be accused of overlooking "the presence of life." And with regard to two fundamental drives, a passage in *The World as Will and Idea* expresses a very similar thought: "What really gives its wonderful and ambiguous character to our life is this, that two diametrically opposed aims constantly cross each other in it, that of the individual will directed toward chimerical happiness in an ephemeral, dreamlike and delusive existence, . . . and that of fate, visibly enough directed toward the destruction of our happiness."[15]

At this point it might be useful to examine the reasons for Schopenhauer's assertion that death is the true aim of life, since it helps to understand his peculiar views on suicide.

Since the Will, of which the world is the manifestation, is a blind and irrational force that operates without ultimate purpose or plan, everything in the world from the simplest physical body to the most complex organism is equally purposeless, engaged in a meaningless struggle for existence. Human life in particular is nothing but "vain striving, inward conflict and continual suffering."[16] It is this view of life that determines Schopenhauer's view of death as "deliverance from this vain, idle and self-contradictory effort." Death is "the moment of liberation from the one-sidedness of individuality, which is not the innermost kernel of our Being, but has to be conceived as an aberration of it."[17] On another occasion he speaks of death as "the great reprimand which the will to live receives through the course of nature; and it may be conceived as a punishment for our existence."[18]

Thus "dying is certainly to be regarded as the true aim of life" because it is the return to "the great All."[19] It is important to realize that this "All" is neither God nor cosmic matter, but Kant's unknowable "thing in itself," which Schopenhauer claims to have discovered as being Will. Another no less important point is that for Schopenhauer man's true nature is indestructible, and that this too is the Will, the "thing in itself," and not the soul. It may appear strange that Schopenhauer goes to considerable length to prove that man's "innermost kernel" is indestructible, and that death is not total annihilation.

The most plausible answer seems to be that, caught between the disgust for life and the fear of death, Schopenhauer created a metaphysics that allowed him not only to justify his pessimism but also to minimize the sting of death. The immortality he finds is, to be sure, not personal survival, but at least it is not absolute extinction. It is the latter that makes Schopenhauer say that "whoever is oppressed with the burden of life has no deliverance to hope from death, and cannot right himself by suicide."[20] Schopenhauer calls suicide "a vain and foolish act" because "the thing in itself remains unaffected by it. . . ."[21] Far from being the result of a failing will to live, suicide, according to Schopenhauer, is "a phenomenon of strong assertion of the will; the suicidal person wills life, and is only dissatisfied with the conditions under which it presents itself to him. He therefore by no means surrenders the will to live, but only life."[22]

It is surprising that Schopenhauer does not seem to realize that what the suicide seeks is deliverance from the burden of his "phenomenal" life and this he fully achieves by killing himself. That his true nature persists may affect adversely the denial of the Will which alone, according to Schopenhauer, would put an end to pain and suffering of the world and of man, but to the individual this can scarcely make any difference.

As we have indicated, Schopenhauer was torn between the feeling that life was a burden and his fear of death, but there is ample evidence to suggest that the latter may have been the stronger force, and that, in the last analysis, not the difficulties of living but the fact of mortality poisoned his enjoyment of life. Not for nothing did he assert that the main task of all religious and philosophical systems was to comfort man with regard to death, and he proudly claimed that his philosophy was perhaps best suited to enable the modern unbeliever "to look death in the face with a quiet glance."

This is perhaps also what Freud expected from his theory of the death drive. There is indeed a modicum of comfort in the thought that something in us actually craves death.

This problem of accepting death, of overcoming the reluctance to die, has in recent times attracted considerable interest on the part of physicians and psychiatrists, particularly in connection with the management of the dying patient. Unfortunately, our understanding of the fear of death is still very inadequate, and the complexity of the phenomena covered by that label has not yet been fully realized, even by most investigators of the psychological aspects of death. The psychoanalytic theory that death fear stems from infantile fears of mutilation, in particular, castration, invites skepticism as an attempt to minimize death. Moreover, as early as 1929 Mary Chadwick pointed out that in religious and penal codes castration represents a lessening of the earlier death penalty, which makes her doubt that fear of castration preceded the fear of death.[23]

Statements like "the fear of death is the obverse of the love of life"[24] are of little help in understanding the nature and origin of the death fear. Biologists caution us against interpreting the concept of self-preservation as if the organism "knows" through some uncanny perceptivity what is good for it in order to remain alive. As Dobzhansky points out, the famous "wisdom of the body" is, indeed, admirable, but "the body is wise chiefly under conditions which the biological species, to which it belongs, encountered in its evolution. Placed in novel conditions, the body loses its wisdom and becomes surprisingly stupid."[25]

And what is this life we love? Certainly not only, if at all, our biological existence. Bertalanffy has pointed out that in addition to the biological life man shares with other animals, he lives in a world of symbols. It is to this "symbolic" life that he is attached, and it is this that he is reluctant to give up. But self-destruction is, according to Bertalanffy, also intimately connected with the symbolic world in which humans live. "The man who kills himself because his life or career or business has gone wrong, does not do so because of the fact that his biological existence and survival are threatened, but rather because of his quasi-needs, that is, his needs on the symbolic level are frustrated."[26] In other words, an individual commits suicide either because his symbolic world demands it (as in the case of a martyr), or because it breaks down.

But what about the fear of death of suicidal people? The investigation of this aspect of the psychodynamics of suicide might help us to understand the nature of the fear of death and show the way of coping with it. Here suicidology has an opportunity of making a contribution toward alleviating an affliction that has beset mankind since the moment *Homo sapiens* first attained the knowledge of the inevitability of death.

But perhaps the mastering of the fear of death is not anymore as important an issue as it used to be. For contemporary man shows distinct signs of having lost the animal *joie de vivre*—the exultation of simply being alive. One could even assert that many—and this includes numbers of those who enjoy physical and social well-being—do not really care whether they are alive or dead. They are prey to the *Un-behagen* of which Freud spoke, and which is not at all mere "discontent," as the English translation has it.[27] It is a feeling of uneasiness, in many instances even a kind of nausea, as described in Jean-Paul Sartre's novel, *La Nausée*. And it is clear that its causes are much more complex than Freud's interpretation that it is due to the suppression of our instinctual drives and the price we have to pay for being civilized. The malady of our age is not so much anxiety as it is "anhedonia," to use William James' term. To combat it is perhaps the true task of a broadly conceived suicidology.

References

[1] Jacques Choron, *Modern Man and Mortality* (New York: Macmillan, 1964).

[2] Jacques Choron, *Death and Western Thought* (New York: Collier-Macmillan, 1963).

[3] Charles W. Wahl, "Suicide as a Magical Act." In E. S. Shneidman and N. L. Farberow (Eds.), *Clues to Suicide* (New York: McGraw-Hill, 1957).

[4] Herbert Hendin, *Suicide and Scandinavia* (New York: Grune and Stratton, 1964).

[5] Jacques Choron, "Suicide and Notions of Death." In Norman L. Farberow (Ed.), *Proceedings of the Fourth International Conference for Suicide Prevention* (Los Angeles: Del Mar, 1968).

[6] Karl A. Menninger, *Man Against Himself* (New York: Harcourt, Brace, 1938).

[7] David Lester, "Psychology and Death," *Continuum*, 1967, No. 5.

[8] Robert E. Litman, "Sigmund Freud on Suicide." In Edwin S. Shneidman (Ed.), *Essays in Self-Destruction* (New York: Science House, 1967).

[9] Norman D. Tabachnik, "Suicide Research and the Death Instinct," *Yale Scientific Magazine,* March, 1967.

[10] Paul Friedman (Ed.), *On Suicide* (New York: International University Press, 1967).

[11] *Modern Man and Mortality.*

[12] Elie Metchnikoff, *Études d'optimisme.* Paris, 1907. (Translated as *Studies in Optimistic Philosophy* by P. Chalmers Mitchell. New York and London: Putnam, 1908.)

[13] Leonardo da Vinci, *The Notebooks of Leonardo da Vinci* (New York: Braziller, 1955).

[14] Sigmund Freud, *New Introductory Lectures on Psychoanalysis* (New York: Norton, 1933).

[15] Arthur Schopenhauer, *The World as Will and Idea,* tr. Haldane and Kemp (London: Routledge and Kegan Paul, 1883), Vol. III, p. 466.

[16] *Op. cit.,* I, 489.

[17] *Op. cit.,* III, 308.

[18] *Op. cit.,* III, 306.

[19] *Op. cit.,* III, 463.

[20] Arthur Schopenhauer, *Parerga und Paralipomena,* second edition (Berlin: 1862), Vol. II, p. 284.

[21] Schopenhauer, *The World as Will and Idea,* I, p. 362.

[22] *Op. cit.,* I, 515

[23] Mary Chadwick, "Notes upon the Fear of Death," *International Journal of Psychoanalysis, 10,* 1929.

[24] G. Stanley Hall, "A Study of Fears," *American Journal of Psychology, 8,* 1896–7.

[25] Theodosius Dobzhansky, *The Biology of Ultimate Concern* (New York: New American Library, 1967), p. 74.

[26] Ludwig von Bertalanffy, "Comments on Aggression." In Irwin G. Sarason (Ed.), *Psychoanalysis and the Study of Behavior* (Princeton, N.J.: Van Nostrand, 1965), p. 114.

[27] Sigmund Freud, *Civilization and its Discontents,* tr. U. Strachey (New York: Norton [Original title: *Unbehagen in der Kultur* in: *Gesammelte Werke* (London: Imago, 1946), Vol. 14]).

2

Louis I. Dublin

Suicide
Prevention

ࠃࠃࠃࠃࠃࠃࠃࠃࠃࠃࠃࠃࠃࠃ

I propose to comment on four aspects of the suicide prevention problem which I believe have bearing on where we may go in the future development of the program.

The change in the climate of interest in suicide prevention. The current interest in suicide prevention in the United States is a fairly new development. Early in this century there was scarcely any interest in this area. Such interest as there was was almost altogether confined to theoretical considerations among the professional groups, particularly the psychiatrists, the clergy, and the lawyers. The general attitude was, on the whole, a negative one. Little, if any, hope was held out for the prevention of suicide. The medical profession, which one might suppose would be most concerned, showed the least interest. The psychiatrists, dominated by Freud and his disciples, were launched into considerations that often led down blind alleys. With rare exceptions, the clergy saw only a sin against God and the lawmakers saw only a crime against the state, which had to be expiated through reprisals in jail or penalties on the next-of-kin. Even the health officers, who had a legal mandate to prevent unnecessary sickness and death, made virtually no provision for the control of suicide.

This was the more surprising because Morselli and Durkheim had already published their classic studies and had outlined some of the possibilities of useful intervention. Nevertheless, there were a few brave spirits who, without special learning or skills, were moved by simple compassion for those in distress and here and there made significant efforts to serve them. Sometimes they were individuals acting independently; sometimes they were representatives of unorthodox religious groups, such as the Salvation Army in England, Germany, and the United States. The Ethical Society of Vienna made an especially valuable demonstration of the possibilities for preventive service. At the same time, studies by the statisticians and sociologists brought together a body of substantial knowledge concerning the victims. They showed that patterns of personality, social relations, and methods existed in the most widely separated places. Their findings outlined the anatomy of suicide or, perhaps better, the epidemiology of suicide, on the basis of which a preventive program might be started.

The discovery of the possibilities of prevention. This apparently was the platform from which the activities of the

National Institute of Mental Heath were launched. Step by step, the work supported by the institute, through grants in support of intensive research and of preventive efforts in various localities, has finally led to what we have today—a nationwide awareness of the importance of suicide as a health and social problem and a determination on the part of our mental health leaders to bring it under control. Out of these sporadic humanitarian efforts grew the confidence that potential suicides could be effectively served. Sometimes these efforts reached as many as several thousand persons a year, each with his own particular problem. Through a process of trial and error it was not long before techniques developed that could be safely followed. In this way the concept of the suicide prevention center took form, although its type of organization varied somewhat from place to place. Soon it was recognized that many social services were often needed and that the center must, therefore, be closely associated with all the official and voluntary health and welfare agencies of the community, acting often as a focal point for the referral of cases to those organizations that could best handle a particular problem. This is essentially the type of agency that has crystallized to serve the needs of suicide prevention in various parts of the country.

The importance of the lay volunteer. The lay volunteer was probably the most important single discovery in the fifty-year history of suicide prevention. Little progress was made until he came into the picture. The lay volunteer had the time and the qualities of character to prove that he cared. With proper training he can make a successful approach to the client, and by his knowledge of the community services available for useful referral he can often tide the client over his crisis. This is not the theoretical construct of an effective organization; it is rather the day-to-day story of a large number of such organizations. It is essentially the story of the

Samaritans of Britain who, in fourteen years, stretched the one-man experiment of Chad Varah into the fifty-four units now operating in virtually every large center of population in England and Scotland, involving thousands of dedicated volunteers and thousands of suicidal persons who come under their care. And it is likewise the story of many suicide prevention centers in the United States and in other parts of the world.

The need for a firm base of support. The recent progress of the movement has clearly been the result of the interest and support of the National Institute of Mental Health. It has made it possible for a few local groups to organize and launch their preventive operations, freed of most of the financial burdens involved. But this support is a hazard as well as a benefit. The National Institute of Mental Health has made it clear that its support has been intended to demonstrate the feasibility of the various efforts. It is, in the last analysis, up to the local communities to take over and finance the organizations which have so fully proved their worth. It has been my hope over the years that the local health departments, supported through local budgets, would take on this function; but, unfortunately, they have not, except in a very few areas. In most instances, the support has been assumed in part, if not altogether, by the local mental health association. The time has now come when the financing of the suicide prevention centers will once and for all have to be placed on a sound financial basis. This means that it must be assumed by the local communities as a part of their regular operating budgets, very much as they support their health departments, mental health clinics, and other governmental agencies. If, as seems likely, the suicide prevention centers of the future will function through the comprehensive mental health clinics, that too would carry with it a guarantee of continuity and of freedom to operate without the embarrassing difficulties of raising funds each year through voluntary contributions from the public. However, this problem of financial support is still wide open for solution and the experience of the next decade will indicate what are probably the most feasible and practicable procedures.

3

Paul Friedman

An
Individual Act

~~~~~~~~~~~~~~~~~~~~~~~

Fifty-eight years after the original symposium on suicide it seems that the original reasons for holding a symposium still obtain today. It is perhaps appropriate to remind ourselves that Europe, at the beginning of this century, allegedly witnessed a resurgence of suicide, especially among young people, and society then sought the causes. Much has been written and many speculations have been made in this

48

effort. One of the most renowned books was the one by A. Baer, *Selbstmord im kindlichen Lebensalter*.[1] Of course, unconscious motivations at that time were not yet considered. Likewise, very little was said about the role of the parents in the suicidal tendencies of their children. We may well hear now that parents today still refuse to assume the responsibility for the suicidal impulses of their children and continue to search for scapegoats in the world outside the family.

Because of the 1910 symposium, a blueprint, as it were, for a half-century of research resulted. It was on that memorable occasion that, for the very first time, the concept that no one kills himself who has not wished to kill another was enunciated by Stekel. And it was Sadger's maxim that no one kills himself or wishes to die who still has hope for love. These intuitive statements acquired credence and more clinical validation later on after Freud's monumental *Mourning and Melancholia* was published. It would take too long to go into all the important topics considered then, but I want to mention a few that are as relevant today as they were in 1910, not necessarily in order of their importance or incidence: family constellation and suicide; desire for revenge; unrequited love; school failures and discrepancy between ability and parental pressure; influence of mass media and publicity on suicide; contagion and imitation. Above all, for the first time, the problem of deep unconscious psychosexual conflicts was brought up as a possible source of guilt, shame, and rage leading to suicidal acts. And we know now that it is no wonder that at puberty there is such a rise of such acts.

I wish it were possible to take a close look at the permissive, overindulgent parents and school authorities so characteristic in this present era of the so-called sexual revolution. By their failure to institute and maintain appropriate and essential control, they have added tremendous confusion to the natural oscillations of adolescence and greatly complicated the

49

process of maturation which, unfortunately, enhances not the libido but the aggressive instinct.

For the moment let us take a further step back in history to note that science does not take a direct course, particularly as far as the problem of suicide is concerned. The nineteenth century, especially the second half, is still looked upon as the first golden era of our thinking on this problem. Great works were published in many parts of the world. The names of Ferri, Morselli, Lombroso, Masaryk and many others are esteemed as the greatest precursors of our thinking today. It is noteworthy that in Italy the study of suicide evolved from the criminological studies on homicide. In France, Esquirol, Brierre de Boismont, L'Espine, Falret, Tissot, and many others conducted important investigations from a psychiatric stand-point. If we can regard Durkheim's epoch-making *Le Suicide* as the culmination of all preceding studies and observations in sociological and criminological thinking, we can as well look upon the symposium of 1910 as the beginning of a new era in psychiatric thinking. (By the way, I still believe that had Durkheim been acquainted with the principles of psychoanalysis, he could right then have made a perfect synthesis between depth psychology and sociology.)

In the middle of this first golden era, however, there was already a certain discontent and criticism directed toward the methods of investigation. In 1885, the Deputy Coroner of the City of London, W. Wynn Westcott, wrote in his concise monograph:

> *The older authors on suicide viewed it from a narra-tive and sentimental point of view, and it is only of late years that it has been the object of any scientific research; but now that a study of suicide as a fact has been instituted, it has fallen almost entirely into a statistical groove, to the neglect of research into the mental state and emotions of the unfortunate indi-viduals who become victims.*[2]

Paul Friedman

I am afraid I may sound like Westcott reincarnated if I come to you with my lamentations. But now I turn again to the symposium of 1910. As I said at the outset, its legacy should be considered a blueprint for research.

More than thirty years ago, in a paper dealing with the psychoanalytic dynamics of suicide,[3] I attempted to show how our resistances had changed only their facade; fundamentally, they remained the same. Following World War II there was an upsurge of interest in suicide research. Never before had there been such an abundance of publications. A broad spectrum of views and hypotheses emerged, ranging from the most primitive ideas handed down to us from generation to generation to the most sophisticated metapsychological speculations applied as ready-made formulas to the solution of the most complex phenomena. We have become accustomed to the indiscriminate use of sophisticated terms and stereotypes. Thus, we have lost ourselves in guessing games and mental acrobatics without examining their clinical value.

The true clinician feels diffident when approaching problems and concepts of a purely speculative nature which transcend the boundaries of clinical experience. Freud, as you may remember, had this attitude throughout life. He warned us against the hasty use of concepts derived from the study of the individual and haphazardly applied to social and community phenomena.

It is regrettable that, after the excellent beginnings of our scientific research, and since the second golden era, from 1910 to the mid-thirties, we have been seesawing in our progress. And now in the middle of what can be the third golden era, thanks to the indefatigable efforts of Shneidman and his colleagues, we must again take a good look at our blueprint. The time has arrived to ask ourselves some searching questions. Do we better understand the individual who is driven to suicide today than we did at that first symposium? Are we better equipped to predict who is about to commit suicide? And finally, are we in a better position to prevent such acts? Our further advances to meaningful answers can come about only through the concerted efforts of all of us with a view toward ultimate pragmatic solutions. Research in depth of the individual in his ontogenetic development must still be our primary concern. I conclude now with a final quotation from Westcott, whose lamentation I can only echo: "Suicide is an individual act, and this point is in danger of being lost sight of in a too absorbing study of general principles."

References

[1] A. Baer, *Selbstmord im kindlichen Lebensalter, Encyklopedisches Handbuch der Heilpädagogik von Danneman,* Schober and Schulze (Halle: Carl Marhold, 1911).

[2] W. Wynn Westcott, *A Social Science Treatise—Suicide: Its History, Literature, Jurisprudence, Causation and Prevention* (London: Lewis, 1885), pp. 68–70.

[3] Paul Friedman, *Sur le Suicide* (Paris: Bibliothèque Psychoanalytique, Les Éditions Derrvel et Steele, 1935).

Robert J. Havighurst

Suicide
and Education

The setting of the 1910 Symposium on Suicide was not much different from today's. There is a pressing concern about suicide among secondary school and university students. Some critics attribute student suicide to the pressure placed by the school on students to succeed in a highly competitive situation where some of them must fail if the standards of the school and their principles of selectivity are to be maintained. There is some evidence, although it is not very clear, of a recent increase in the suicide rate among adolescents and especially among students.

Consequently, a group of informed and dispassionate men are gathered to discuss the problem of suicide, its causes and its prevention.

The two panels are somewhat similar, but not explicitly so. A teacher of classics led off with the main presentation of the problem in 1910. He defended the schools against the charge that they were causing an increase of suicides. A number of psychologists and psychiatrists commented from their experience on the problem of suicide. One of them, "Dr. Karl Molitor"—a pseudonym for Carl Furtmüller—discussed the possibilities for suicide prevention in a more humane or "progressive" kind of school. He suggested that the school could and should use its supportive potential to reduce rather than to intensify the psychic stress that may lead to suicide. School, he said, should treat the boy better than life will treat the man.

Notably lacking in the 1910 symposium was the sociologist—the student of human behavior as influenced by the group.

The basic theme of this contemporary symposium has two parts: first, to determine the causes and correlates of suicide; second, to determine what can be done to reduce or to prevent suicide.

When investigating the causes and correlates of suicide, we must first consider the social situation. It is immediately clear from an examination of the data on the incidence of suicide that the suicide rate is related to the social situation. The evidence indicates variation in suicide rate among contemporary societies, and also among historical epochs and between historical episodes. Although suicide is a personal act, it is very much influenced by the location of a person in social space and time.

Second, we must consider the personal situation. Since different people who are in very similar social situations have different probabilities of committing suicide, there must be a personal variable active in suicide. Suicide is an act of the self, or the ego.

Third, we must consider the interaction of the personal and the social situations. Any useful theory of suicide must deal with interaction of the self, the society, and the body. The 1910 symposium neglected the society. Durkheim neglected the self. One can read all of Durkheim on suicide and it appears as though all of suicide depends on status and society.

Until fairly recently, students of suicide neglected the body—the biological aspects. There have been some attempts, of course, but social scientists have tended to put the body aside. On the other hand, it is clear that suicide rates do depend somewhat on dispositions within the body. Some measure of the usefulness of this contemporary symposium is the extent to which it brings the three causal elements—self, body, and society—together.

Some interesting social correlates of suicide follow:

First, there are significant male-female differences. Males commit suicide more frequently than females in all contemporary societies that we know about, and at all ages. Since there are substantially more male deaths than female deaths in the first half of life, the suicide rate (as number of suicides per 100,000 living persons) is about three times as high for males as for females, and has been so in the United States at least since the 1910–20 decade. On the other hand, many more females than males *attempt* suicide. The greatest male-female difference in suicide rates occurs in the age period from fifteen to twenty-four, while twenty-five to thirty-nine appears to be the age when female suicides reach their highest proportions to male suicides.

On the Nature of Suicide

Examination of age differences offers some interesting patterns. The suicide rate rises with age. For instance, the rate for white American males in 1940 rose from 22 per 100,000 population for ages twenty-five to thirty-four, to sixty-five per 100,000 for ages seventy-five to eighty-four. One factor that probably contributes to the high figures for people past sixty is the growing incidence of incurable disease and pain. Here we see the state of the body operating to affect the suicide rate.

Statistics reveal variation among countries or societies. Suicide is judged differently in different societies. For reasons that undoubtedly are complicated, there is a wide variety of suicide rates among modern countries. Countries with high suicide rates were (1950) Austria, Denmark, Switzerland, West Germany, France, and Japan (all above 15 per 100,000). Countries with intermediate suicide rates were the United Kingdom, Australia, New Zealand, the United States, Canada, Uruguay, South Africa (Europeans only), Italy, and the Netherlands (6 to 12 per 100,000). Countries with low suicide rates were Ireland, Egypt, Chile, El Salvador, Mexico, Colombia, and Costa Rica (below 5 per 100,000).

For the years of adolescence and of early adulthood (ages fifteen to twenty-four) the order of countries is slightly different. Those with high suicide rates are Austria (18); Japan (20); and Denmark (23). Intermediate rates are found in the United States (10); West Germany (12); and South Africa (13). Countries with low suicide rates for young people are the United Kingdom (4); the Netherlands (4); France (4); Canada (4); and Australia (6).

There appears to be substantial variation of suicide rates by historical epoch, though this is hard to establish in the absence of systematic death records. The data for European countries have been fairly consistent since the early nineteenth century, and these data indicate a substantial increase in suicide rates for most European countries between 1840 and 1925. However, Denmark and Norway reversed this trend.

There are sharp local and temporary increases in the suicide rate that can be traced to specific causes. For example, the publication of Goethe's *Sorrows of Young Werther* is said to have caused a wave of youthful suicides. More striking still is the outbreak of suicides on the Japanese volcano-island of Mihara-Yama. A girl of nineteen, Kiyoko Matsumoto, took a boat to this small island, about a two-hour trip from Tokyo, climbed up the side of the mountain to the crater's edge, and threw herself in. This occurred in February, 1933. The newspapers played it up. In the remaining ten months of 1933, 143 people jumped into the crater. A steamship company established a thriving tourist business carrying sightseers to the island from Tokyo. In one particular day there were six committed suicides and twenty-five attempts. The next year, 1934, there were 167 suicides on the island. In 1935, the government took steps to screen passengers on the boat and stopped the suicide fad.

During World War II, from 1940 to about 1943, the suicide rate dropped among the warring nations in Europe, and then rose again. The rate took a sharp upturn in Austria in 1945 presumably because of the stresses and strains of a losing war and occupation by enemy troops.

Suicide rates in the United States are also related to socioeconomic status and to race. Lower-status men have a slightly higher suicide rate than middle-class men.

For each of four socioeconomic levels as determined by occupation (for men aged twenty to sixty-four), a "standardized mortality ratio" was computed for each of the various causes of death. The standardized mortality ratio is the ratio of actual number of deaths due to a specific cause to the expected number of deaths due to this cause if they had been

57

distributed equally over the four occupational groups and the white and nonwhite groups. The standardized mortality ratio rises from 86 for the middle-class group of technicians, managers, and proprietors, to 147 for the lower working-class group of laborers. Among nonwhites there is a somewhat similar trend, although there were not enough nonwhite deaths in the highest level to provide a base for a reliable ratio.

It seems clear also that the suicide rate for nonwhites is below that for whites, on a given occupational level. The suicide rate for nonwhites was below that for whites in 1965 at all ages and both sexes, except for ages fifteen to twenty-four, where the difference is probably not reliable.

It may be said that suicide may result from external social factors, internal psychological factors, and internal biological factors. Since these three categories are always interacting with each other, the causes of suicide are likely to be combinations of them. It turns out that bodily distress, such as intractable pain, is not a very frequent immediate cause. Also, there is no longer any substantial belief that suicide is caused by some pathological condition in a gland, such as the thymus.

External social or cultural factors must operate significantly to account for the wide variations of suicide rates among modern societies and between subgroups within modern societies. For example, it seems probable that religious belief is a factor, as suggested by the low rates in Muslim countries and in most Catholic countries. The variation of suicide rate with socioeconomic status also suggests a cultural or social cause.

Durkheim gives some useful clues to social causation when he speaks of the inverse relation between suicide rate and the extent of external social constraints and expectations that operate on people; and also when he speaks of the inverse relation between suicide rate and the extent of social interaction in a society. A number of instances of variation of suicide rate with change of the social situation have been explained on the basis of Durkheim's theory, which possibly can account for the great differences in suicide rate between the Netherlands, Belgium, and Switzerland. These are examples of societies with quite similar levels of political and religious and family integration, yet they produce substantially different rates of suicide.

Considerably more useful, it seems to me, is the attempt to explain suicide rates by the way people in a society learn to cope with aggression, inward (against the self) or outward (against others). Stekel's statement is important: "No one kills himself who did not want to kill another, or, at least, wish death to another."[1]

To understand more of the etiology of suicide, one may relate it to homicide and study the ratio of suicide to homicide. Assuming that there is a considerable amount of frustration in the lives of people in all societies and that frustration produces aggression, why do people in some social groups direct this aggression against themselves and commit suicide, while people in other cultures or social groups direct their aggression against others and commit homicide?

Perhaps we can say that each cultural group teaches its members to cope with aggression in a way that is acceptable to the culture. Thus the relative levels of suicide and homicide rates reflect the ways people have learned to cope with their aggressive impulses.

Using this kind of consideration, one can begin to understand the high homicide and low suicide rates in Colombia, Mexico, and El Salvador, in contrast to the high suicide and low homicide rates of most of the West European countries. But this seems too simple to account for the low suicide and homicide rates of Ireland and Egypt and Chile. People in these countries must experience about as much frustration as people in the other countries.

Again, this kind of consideration helps one to under-

59

stand the social class differences in suicide and homicide rates among men in the United States. It may be expected that lower-status people experience more frustration than middle-class people, and therefore have higher combined rates of suicide and homicide, as they do in fact. It may also be suggested that lower-status people have less effective control over aggressive impulses than middle-class people have, and therefore both suicide and homicide rates are higher for lower-class people. Something similar seems to happen in relation to social class among Negroes, but the American Negro subculture seems to teach its people more acting-out of their aggressions. It would be expected that the Negro figures would shift in the direction of the white figures as Negroes and whites come together in work, worship, and play.

The 1910 symposium is entitled "On suicide—with particular reference to suicide among young students." It was alleged at the time that there was a resurgence of suicide in Europe, especially among young people. In the opening paper of the symposium, David Oppenheim cites the only statistical evidence that was available—the Prussian statistics. He says:

> By the second half of the eighteenth century, the cases were already so numerous that they demanded statistical registration. In Prussia, statistics relating to suicide in youthful years go back to 1749. The series clearly shows an upward trend. Between 1883 and 1905, the suicide rate for young people rose from 7.02 to 8.26 per 100,000. Fortunately, the figures do not show the same steady rate of increase as the adult suicide rate. There are sharp drops which are leveled out by gradual increases.
>
> The causes of an evil of such range and antiquity cannot be narrowly defined either temporally or spatially. Therefore, they cannot be ascribed to educational institutions of recent origin that are localized in Austria. But even if we assume that harsh discipline at school is in fact as antagonistic to life impulses as many crit-

*ics assert, how are we to explain that suicide among
the young is increasing although the principle of
gentleness toward the weak reigns in all our public in-
stitutions, including our schools?*

*But even the increase in the number of student sui-
cides is not beyond doubt. Unfortunately, we have
statistical material not for Austrian, but only for Prussian schools. But these are surely not milder than ours;
corporal punishment, completely forbidden in our
country, is permitted in Prussia up to the top grade of
the secondary school. Despite this strict discipline, the
number of pupils at all levels who committed suicide
was no higher in 1905 than in 1883—fifty-eight for
each of these years.*[2]

Oppenheim's search for objective data deserves to be
repeated, and a limited search by a contemporary student indicates, as did Oppenheim's, that the journalistic treatments
of suicide tend to distort the facts. For instance, the American
popular writer, Max Gunther, citing suicide rates in the
United States for 1954 and 1964 in the age groups ten to
fourteen and fifteen to nineteen, said that the rates are rising
"each year for several years: gradually, but perceptibly,
more."[3]

From the data on suicide rates for the United States
at several dates in recent years, it appears possible that there
has been a slight rise in the suicide rate for ages fifteen to
twenty-four, but this rise is no greater than the increase in the
twenty-five to thirty-four range. At present, about four per
cent of all deaths of youths aged fifteen to nineteen are due to
suicide, and about 6.5 per cent of deaths in the twenty to
twenty-four range are suicides. The significance of these figures,
as well as their causes, is a matter of disagreement.

The British anthropologist, Edmund Leach, in lectures that he gave for the British Broadcasting Corporation in
1967, had some unkind remarks for the British educational
system, which he said becomes "viciously competitive" from

the age of ten upwards. After saying that the old British system of class stratification based on hereditary wealth has been partly replaced by a new class system based on achieved status, he continued:

> *Simultaneously our educational system has developed into an entirely ruthless machine for the elimination of the unworthy. Suicide and mental breakdown are now so common in student populations that they are almost taken for granted....*
>
> *For most of us education is an instrument of war, a weapon by which the individual beats down his competitors and defends himself against adversity. I assure you, I do not exaggerate.*[4]

Such opinions are being stated on this side of the Atlantic also, and generally with the same broad sweep and the same lack of objective evidence. It seems to me that Leach and his American counterparts do exaggerate.

Among the adult population in the United States the suicide rate is inversely related to the amount of education. That is, people with more than average education are less likely to commit suicide than people with less than average education. This is so for men in relation to occupational status and therefore so for educational status.

However, it is likely that college students have a higher suicide rate than noncollege students of the same age. For instance, Philip Werdell claimed that about a third of deaths among college students were due to suicide.[5] (For the age group twenty to twenty-four in 1965, about 7 per cent of all deaths were due to suicide.) The only cause of death among college students that exceeded suicide was accidents. This may seem to be a high rate for suicide, but we should remember that the death rate is very low among young people, with death from disease being very infrequent. Self-inflicted death is bound to appear relatively high in a population that does

62

not suffer much from disease or from homicide. Young people who do not go to college are much more likely to die of homicide than of suicide.

The question of greatest practical importance is whether one form of education can reduce or prevent suicide, while another form of education may encourage suicide. Or, to put it another way, given the fact of interaction of the social environment and the individual psyche in the causation of suicide, can the school or college environment be modified in the direction of reducing suicide, or in the direction of increasing suicide?

On this question we may refer to the remarks of Sigmund Freud at the 1910 symposium. After hearing Oppenheim's defense of the secondary schools, Freud said:

> *A secondary school should achieve more than not driving its pupils to suicide. It should give them a desire to live and should offer them support and backing at a time of life at which the conditions of their development compel them to relax their ties with their parental home and their family. It seems to me indisputable that schools fail in this, and in many respects fall short of their duty of providing a substitute for the family and of arousing interest in life and in the world outside. This is not a suitable occasion for a criticism of secondary schools in their present shape; but perhaps I may emphasize a single point. The school must never forget that it has to deal with immature individuals who cannot be denied a right to linger at certain stages of development and even at certain disagreeable ones. The school must not take on itself the inexorable character of life: it must not seek to be more than a game of life.[6]*

We may presume that Freud would have the secondary school be at one and the same time more supportive of young people as they prepare to take on adult roles, and also more affirmative of the values of the society to which they are about to commit their lives. Erikson has spoken of the two sources of weakness in adolescents—lack of self-esteem and lack of social fidelity.[7] Education can help adolescents to gain self-assurance presumably by helping them see themselves as players in the game of preparing for life roles rather than by making them see themselves as already grown up, with full responsibility for success or failure in the serious business of life.

We are familiar with the change that psychiatrists report among their youthful patients. They encounter less anxiety of a psychosexual sort today than they did one and two generations ago, but they see more anxiety over identity diffusion—the failure of the adolescent to define for himself clearly and effectively the adult role he wants to fill.

Insofar as anxiety is related to suicide, we may see here the interaction of the social-environmental with the psychological in the causation of suicide. In a former day, the society taught young people to be anxious and to feel guilty over their sexual feelings and activities. Today the society permits young people to be more relaxed about sex but it makes the choice of a career more complicated for both sexes and it exposes young people more frankly to the shortcomings of our society and to the negative aspects of human personality, thus causing them to suffer from lack of social fidelity and lack of self-assurance.

The mood of our society includes frankness in formerly taboo areas, self-criticism, and skepticism. Youth are exposed to this mood very directly through the mass media (television, cinema, paperback literature, and so on). They read such books as Salinger's *Catcher in the Rye* and Golding's *Lord of the Flies;* they are encouraged to read such literature by high school literature teachers who represent the mood of society. These books are true portrayals of a part of human nature—an unpleasant part, and not the whole truth, by any means. Perhaps these are more accurate than the literature that adolescents read a generation or more ago— *Rebecca of Sunnybrook Farm, Strive and Succeed.* Furthermore, the sober and realistic writing about the dangers of nuclear war and the difficulties of international control of armaments give young people an ample picture of the immorality of national policies. Boys and girls are shown the seamy side of personal and political life and then asked to commit themselves to social loyalty.

At the same time, boys and girls are confronted with the tasks of making good in school, of choosing an occupation, of establishing relations with the opposite sex; and these tasks are set for them a year or two earlier than they were a generation or two ago, due to the social forces making for social precocity in the middle-class part of society.

Under these circumstances, it is not surprising that contemporary middle-class youth show a considerable degree of self-doubt and lack of confidence in the political and economic structure of modern society. It is not surprising that a privatistic life is preferred to one of greater social commitment. Boys find it difficult to make up their minds what occupation they will prepare for. Some of them engage in a kind of sit-down strike against the academic demands made on them by school or college. Their fathers wonder why sons are so ingrown and uncertain, as compared with the greater assurance and task orientation they remember as normal for their generation. There is not so much concern about girls, since they are not expected to show the degree of instrumental activism expected of boys. With them there is more concern about their sex role, and about the place of sexual activity in the life of a teen-aged girl.

What can the secondary school do to help young

people develop more fidelity to their society and more confidence in themselves? Such a school program might contain the following elements:

1. Opportunity for service to society. A variety of projects during the school year and during the summer for improvement of the school, the local community, and the wider community. This will lead to a commitment to social welfare and a faith in the improvability of society.

2. Positively oriented study of society. Stress in courses in social studies on the achievement of modern society in solving problems of public health, poverty, educational, and economic opportunity, and the building of an interdependent world.

3. Use of adult models who demonstrate both self-esteem and social fidelity. Choice of teachers who are socially optimistic, active, and oriented toward the improvement of society. There is a greater chance in the future for the selection of teachers with appropriate personalities for certain age groups as the teacher shortage decreases and opportunity increases to select the better ones. The use of biography in literature and the social studies could stress heroes with these positive qualities. Currently, a new set of biographical films is being produced which centers around the lives of contemporary people who are making positive contributions to the life of society, who have faith in the improvability of this society and lead personal lives that can serve as models for youth.

Good education strikes a balance between analysis and affirmation. Perhaps the education of middle-class children in recent years has been too strong on analysis and too weak on affirmation. Perhaps we should remember, though, that the sensitive, intelligent adolescent who is declining to settle for a simple, positive identity, has a valuable faculty for criticism and nonconformity, very much needed in our society.

Perhaps this person needs these years to grow in his

powers of analysis and social criticism, even though he may be somewhat unhappy and he may make his family uncomfortable. The kind of person whom we wish to educate will not see the world in one color or parochial perspective nor will he despair because of the complexity of the world and the depravity of human nature. He will have an inner strength, an integrity of mind and spirit, combined with a broad understanding of this world that will enable him to work effectively at the task of making history.

References

1 Wilhelm Stekel, in Paul Friedman (Ed.), *On Suicide* (New York: International Universities Press, 1967).
2 David Oppenheim, in Friedman, *op. cit.*
3 Max Gunther, "Why Children Commit Suicide," *Saturday Evening Post,* June 17, 1967.
4 Edmund Leach, *Reith Lectures* (New York: Oxford University Press, 1968).
5 Philip Werdell, article in *The Moderator,* October, 1966.
6 Sigmund Freud, in Friedman, *op. cit.*
7 Erik H. Erikson, *Childhood and Society,* Revised edition (New York: Norton, 1964).

5

Karl Menninger

Expression
and Punishment

ᘏᘏᘏᘏᘏᘏᘏᘏᘏᘏᘏᘏᘏᘏᘏ

This symposium is a tribute to the indefatigability
and the dedication of those who took seriously what quite a
few of us were saying many years ago, namely that the incidence of suicide will be reduced only when the public rec-
ognizes it as a social problem, as a psychological problem,
and as a medical problem, rather than as a moral problem
and a disgrace to be covered up, regretted, and forgotten.

It is a curious thing that the element of shame, the

idea of the disgracefulness of it, became attached to suicide, because that idea does not seem to apply in many countries. We owe, after all, a considerable debt for our cultural development to Rome. Suicide was not a disgrace in Roman times. The suicide of Lucretia was for years held up as a model of something brave and virtuous, and so remains for these two thousand years, and yet the most superficial examination of it makes one wonder why that ever came to be. Why should one be ashamed of being so overwhelmed? What good did her suicide do? Whom did it punish? I doubt if Tarquin cared very much whether she killed herself or not. Whom did it reward? I doubt if her huband was so pleased to come home and find her corpse. Whom did it inspire? Do girls need to be inspired to avoid rape? And, is it inspiring that Lucretia felt badly enough about it to kill herself? Did she really think that her husband would rather have her dead than forcibly dishonored, as she called it? Was it not bad enough to be raped without having to be killed? Did her suicide accomplish anything? Why should it be held up in poetry and in history and in the thinking of many people as a certain kind of brave act?

I suggest this because I am trying to bring into the arena of discussion of suicide some different flavor than we have heard so far. I want you to think about some of the suicides that we see in the pages of history and of which Henry Murray and M. D. Faber so well reminded us in their fine articles in *Essays in Self-Destruction.*[1]

Suicides have been variously thought of as stemming from bravery and cowardice, from fear and from patriotism, from wisdom, from fright, from pride, from envy, from loneliness, from self-punishment, and especially from the desire to punish someone else. Was Romeo's suicide called for? It was about time for retribution to reach a man who had crashed a party, seduced a child, insulted a dignified family, slain a relative of his infatuation, upset a city for the sake of his eroticism, and altogether caused sorrow and distress to scores of people. Other lovers in this world have been aroused and impetuous, others have been zealous, but is it necessary to leave a trail of blood and turmoil behind one and end up with a double suicide in order to be thought of as the world's most romantic, if not the most clumsy, lover?

Romeo's self-destruction began long before his last piece of ill-managed impulsivity. This is certainly one of the things which the study of the scientific determinants of suicide, which Freud did so much to further, has taught us. The romanticizing of suicide is one error; the scotomatizing of it is another. We shut our eyes to the suicide behavior of our friends who drink too much, or drive too fast, or drink and then drive; we shut our eyes to the behavior of our friends who smoke too much or eat too much. And the manufacturing and stockpiling of totally unnecessary world-destroying explosives goes on ever more rapidly, ever more blindly and more stupidly and more ominously.

With all the accidents, wars, riots, crimes, violence, and sicknesses of the earth, perhaps suicide is an outdated subject for scientific interest. Perhaps some may think that those who quietly do away with themselves are doing the wisest thing. Maybe the world is a hopeless place and we are doomed to more or less quiet desperation, if not violent extinction. It has always been noticed that in times of war, suicide and crime rates diminish, and if there are more murders there are somewhat fewer suicides and vice versa, but this is no longer the case. The incidence of outright suicide has not greatly diminished in spite of the extravagant array of crime and war and other violence around the earth.

In addition, partial, chronic and focalized forms of self-destruction seem rather to be multiplying than to be diminishing. The greater social self-destructiveness that occurs at this moment does not even have this redeeming feature, which previous wars—World War I and World War II—did have. There are some who see the whole Vietnam warfare as a nightmare, as a piece of wholesale social suicide, the waging of a broadside self-destruction by several groups in a war that, of course, no one can win. The net result is destruction. Which, asks the conscious objector, is the more self-destructive, to march off to war to kill or be killed by someone I do not know and never saw, or to stay home and be imprisoned by my own fellow citizens for protesting? Are not both of these courses of conduct open to me self-destructive?

I think it is important to distinguish between suicide as a form of death and suicide as an attempted expression of something within one: helplessness, desperation, fear, and the other emotions. In the past few years I have tried to say that all symptoms that we recognize in psychiatry, all the things we have considered in the past to be evidences of illness except those directly dependent upon brain lesions and poisons, are all devices that are actually sacrifices offered to avert suicide and the dreadful decision that there is nowhere else to go.

If one thinks in these terms, one gets a new view of what we ordinarily call sickness, or certainly of many sicknesses, mental and physical. One would then see that the development of symptoms is a struggle for health, a struggle toward recovery, an effort to avert something which is even worse than that to which one must submit in order to escape it. The organism says, anything rather than suicide, anything rather than give up the most precious thing of all, namely my life. Sickness, even neurosis, even crime, but not that awful oblivion, that awful ultimate nothingness. The suicidal gesture is thus a cry not only of distress, not only a cry for help, not only a prayer, but it is a pleading: I want to live; help me find a way to live. We say that where there is life there is hope. In a sense, one could say that where there is hope there may be life.

On the Nature of Suicide

Each year of my life I am more impressed with the wisdom of some of the great thinkers of ancient times. I am always moved by the poignancy of those famous and beautiful words of Isaiah. Counseling those of us who have emerged from our struggles sufficiently to be able to help others, the spokesman of God says, "Comfort my people, speak tenderly and tell them their punishment is ended." In other words, tell them they have more than paid for their sins, real and imaginary. And right at this point, the stone age of theological thinking terminated—or should have. Punishment died—or should have. Unfortunately, the psychological makeup of mankind is such that in the cultural socialization of aggression, too much of it was taken up by corruptible or naive superegos which could not distinguish between appropriate penalty and vengeful punishment. The unconscious yen for squaring matters by punishing someone was so insistent that it lasted through the influence of the early Greek thinkers and through the influence of the early Christian period, either of which might have corrected it, on up to such great thinkers as Kant. This notion that you can square matters by punishing someone, that punishment evens things up and then the world can go on, if only we find a victim, still persists.

If someone can be civilized out of this primitive, obsolete, immoral, self-destructive compulsion to punish someone, then I think that suicide in all its forms, chronic and acute, direct and indirect, projected and introjected, will begin to diminish. When the idea of punishment can be extracted from our archaic and disgraceful criminal law as it has been from intelligent child rearing, the public will no longer feel it is necessary or even permissible to punish itself or its offending fellow man. We can then begin to listen to Isaiah of over two thousand years ago: no punishment for children, no punishment for offenders, no punishment for ourselves, except the regret—which, in a way, is a mild intellectual punishment—that we did not have more wisdom, more kindness, and more hope a long time ago.

So, when we think of this meeting and the progress on suicide that it represents, we can take some courage and say, like Galileo—although it has been painfully slow—it moves, it moves, it does move.

Reference

[1] Edwin S. Shneidman (Ed.), *Essays in Self-Destruction* (New York: Science House, 1967).

Erwin Stengel

A Matter of
Communication

I should like to confine myself to two topics on which I may be able to say something that has not been said before. The first is the historical status of the 1910 symposium. The second is the approach to suicidal acts with which I have been particularly concerned. The two aspects on which I propose to comment are not unrelated, because part of recent suicide research has been focused on problems touched upon in the 1910 symposium but not further pursued.

74

Erwin Stengel

The 1910 symposium on suicide had a sorry fate. It was known to very few people until 1929, when Paul Federn published a report on it in a special number of the *Zeitschrift fur psychoanalytische Paedagogik,* a periodical for the application of psychoanalysis to education, written for educators rather than for psychoanalysts and psychiatrists. That journal appeared for about ten years only and was little known outside Austria and Germany. The special number in which Federn's report appeared contained fourteen articles on suicide. It conveyed the views on suicide held by psychoanalysts at the time. It is remarkable that they appeared in that particular periodical and not in one of the main psychoanalytic journals. To the English-speaking world, the symposium became available only in 1967, both in Volume II of the Minutes of the Vienna Society and in the translation *On Suicide,* edited by Paul Friedman and based on a version published in 1910.[1] Thus, it took the symposium fifty-seven years to be translated into English, only two years longer than it had taken for the translation of Durkheim's monograph.

The oblivion into which the symposium fell was no doubt due to its association with the first secession from the Freudian circle, that of Adler, who took a leading part in the discussion, to be followed later by that of Stekel, another very active participant. The fact that the symposium on suicide was associated with these traumatic events in the history of psychoanalysis seems to have had an inhibiting effect on psychoanalytic suicide research, which for a very long time was dominated solely by Freud's contribution. Many valuable cues, in which the symposium is so rich, were not followed up. It remained the only occasion when suicide was the main topic of discussion among psychoanalysts in Europe. I am not aware that it has ever been one of the main subjects in an International Psychoanalytic Congress.

To me the 1910 symposium has a nostalgic poignancy

which it may not have for anyone else here. Professor David Ernst Oppenheim, who so gallantly defended the teachers in the discussion of the causes of suicides among students, was my classics master. Of all the teachers from my grammar school days he stands out in my memory the most vividly. He endeavored, with enormous and infectious enthusiasm, to convey to us the greatness and beauty of classical literature. It was not surprising that he felt drawn to Freud, whose cultural orientation owed so much to the classics. When I sat at Professor Oppenheim's feet, I had, of course, no idea that he was interested in anything other than Homer and Horace, nor had I any idea of Freud and psychoanalysis.

The psychoanalytic contribution to suicide research has been mainly concerned with the intrapsychic dynamics of self-destructive tendencies. This has been both its strength and its limitation. It has until recently not concerned itself with the external world, apart from those objects which by introjection become parts of the inner world. Zilboorg's discovery of the role of the broken home in suicide proneness was a brilliant observation deduced from the study of intrapsychic processes and confirmed by clinical and epidemiological studies.[2]

Like suicide research in general, the psychoanalytic approach has been exclusively retrospective. It has closely followed the rules of the post-mortem autopsy. It has yielded many valuable insights and will no doubt continue to so do, but nobody reading through the psychoanalytic, psychiatric, and sociological literature on suicide would gather that the vast majority of suicidal acts do *not* result in death. I mean intentional acts more or less clearly aiming at self-destruction. What happens to the introjected object the suicidal act aims at killing and to the various conflicts of which it is meant to be the final solution if the individual survives? What is the life expectation of people who have made suicide attempts? And what is the expectation of suicide? And what effect, if any, has the suicidal act on the individual's inner life, life situation, and interpersonal relationships?

The fact that these simple, obvious, and inescapable questions have until recently not been asked is a remarkable phenomenon, and it requires a good deal of explaining. Perhaps these questions have not been asked because we were not ready for them. It is only recently that psychoanalysts have turned from the exclusive preoccupation with intrapsychic processes to the study of interpersonal relations; that epidemiology has taught us that we cannot go on talking as if all those who perform suicidal acts kill themselves and ignore the vast majority who survive. It has also made it incumbent on the students of suicidal behavior to carry out cohort studies and to follow people who committed suicidal acts to the end of their natural lives. It is here that a center of suicidology whose research projects are not limited in time and do not depend on individuals can do invaluable work.

The realization that every individual is part of one or more social units has led me to study of the various effects of the suicidal acts, fatal and nonfatal, on those close to the actor and victim. What are those effects in case of a fatal outcome? They have much in common with those of bereavement, but they are more intense than the typical grief reactions. There is an upsurge of posthumous love associated with guilt feelings and self-reproach for not having cared and loved enough. There is ample evidence that these effects play a part in the conscious and unconscious motivations of suicidal acts. By making others feel and appear guilty, suicides bring about changes in attitudes of individuals and of society as a whole. They convey a message from the victim to those close to him. We have already heard a good deal about the aggressive contents of this message.

The effects of suicidal attempts, that is, of nonfatal suicidal acts, are even more complex. Those close to the attempter, and sometimes society as a whole, tend to behave as they feel they ought to behave had the outcome been fatal. The appeal effect, or appeal function, of the suicidal attempt derives from this reaction, irrespective of whether or not such an effect was intended. This is why I am against the division of suicidal acts into those with and without a communicative function. Any such act, intended or not, conveys a message. It must be expected and can be predicted either to end in death or to act as an appeal for help. Both these eventualities are inherent in every suicidal act. Therefore, to divide suicidal acts into those aiming at self-destruction and those meant to be cries for help is, in my opinion, mistaken. They are not either one or the other but both at the same time.

Most people who commit acts of self-damage with more or less conscious self-destructive intent do not want either to live or to die, but to do both at the same time— usually one more than the other.

Most suicidal acts are manifestations of risk-taking behavior. They are gambles. The danger to life depends on the relationship between self-destructive and life-preserving, contact-seeking tendencies, and on a variety of other factors, some of which are outside the control of the individual. Uncertainty of outcome is not a contamination of the genuine suicidal act, but rather one of its inherent qualities.

Many workers have tried to classify suicidal acts according to various criteria. Obviously, people who take no risk, subjectively, ought not to be included among the suicidal acts. But we must beware of viewing suicidal acts as rational undertakings based on clear intentions. Their purpose and outcome are as uncertain and varied as those of aggressive acts directed against other persons. Whether such acts, if their outcome is fatal, are judged to be homicide, manslaughter, or mishap depends on all sorts of conditions. It is difficult to decide whether those acts are aimed at "cessation," "interruption" or "altered continuation"—to use Shneidman's terms —of the victim's experiences and physical condition. At any rate, homicides undertaken with the clear intention of ending another person's life are rare. So let us not be too exacting and restrictive in classifying suicidal acts. If determination to achieve a fatal outcome was the main criterion of suicidal and homicidal acts, only few would qualify.

Earlier I referred to the psychodynamic repercussions of suicidal acts on people close to the victim. How do those effects manifest themselves in psychological and social terms if, as occurs in the vast majority of suicidal acts, he survives? Elsewhere I have listed several categories of changes they may bring about in the attempter's psychological and social conditions.[3] Briefly, the suicidal attempt calls forth a variety of helpful responses which usually transform the individual's life situation, if only temporarily. The relationship of those responses to the suicidal behavior pattern is so typical and so general that the sequence of events is reminiscent of the innate release mechanisms described by the ethologists. If that sequence of events fails to take place, that is, if the suicidal attempt fails to bring about any change in the conditions which led up to it, an early repetition is to be expected, possibly with a fatal outcome. It is important therefore in every suicidal attempt to ask what change it has achieved. This is why a purely intrapsychic appraisal is not enough. It ignores the communicative function of the suicidal act. If it is fatal, it is a final message: if it is not fatal, it is part of a dialogue. And you cannot understand a dialogue if you take notice of one participant only.

References

[1] Paul Friedman (Ed.), *On Suicide* (New York: International Universities Press, 1967).

[2] Gregory Zilboorg, "Considerations on Suicide, with Particular Reference to That of the Young," *American Journal of Orthopsychiatry*, *7*, 1937, 15–31.

[3] Erwin Stengel, *Suicide and Attempted Suicide* (Baltimore: Penquin Books, 1964).

7

Lawrence Kubie

A Complex Process

I am going to focus on the rather peculiar and special difficulties of doing scientific research in the area of studying self-injury including self-extinction, without focusing exclusively on self-extinction. This demands clear, tough thinking. I shudder whenever I hear a sentence that begins, "Suicide is . . ." We know that there is such a thing as people ending their own lives and there is such an event as suicide which can be studied, but "suicide" is an abstraction made from generalizations about many extraordinarily subtly different processes—even though the end result has a unique constancy with uniquely consistent consequences. This last fact deludes us into thinking that all these are one phenomenon. This is my main theme.

What is most extraordinary about these phenomena is man's unique ability to deny realities, even the reality of death, and, most particularly, the reality of his own death. And related to this is a somewhat overlooked tendency to turn our minds away from the vast symbolic value of reality, the symbolic values of death and life. As a result of these confusions in our thinking, we tend to lump all self-injuring acts together with those that have extinction as their consequence and as their goal. And yet, any one of us who sees anything of clinical work knows better than this.

To assume that every act of self-injury has self-extinction as its goal is a serious fallacy. Sometimes, the conscious and unconscious goals may be precisely the reverse. For example, patients not infrequently are released from hospital care before they are ready for this and it happens that they struggle desperately to return to the hospital. If the hospital becomes obstinate and defensive and dismisses the patient's appeal as manifestation of hospitalism or dependency, the desperation increases until the patient may take overdoses of medications or slash a wrist. Such efforts are not efforts to die but to live. This is only one example of many similar errors which are made if one assumes that every patient who injures himself is planning to kill himself. Many of the examples are much subtler. When such an effort fails it becomes possible to make an intensive retrospective study of the person, thus to determine what the real motives have been. Unfortunately, such patients are not studied often enough or intensively enough, but when they are studied, a wide range of conscious, unconscious, and preconscious goals comes to light.

Many acts of self-injury, which are lumped together under the concept of suicide, do not have self-extinction as their goal. The first thing we have to find out is when they do and when they do not. This is by no means easy to do. This is one of the important areas of great difficulty of research in the field. One of the things that is obvious is that people who do survive are a weighted sample. We do not know how truly representative a sample they are. And then we are dependent upon their own retrospective testimony, testimony which inevitably must be distorted in many ways: by repression, by guilt, by almost dream-like elaborations, sometimes elaborations which occur during periods in which they may be toxic from medication or exsanguination. The data which they give us are important data, but they are dependable only if they are studied with extremely critical care.

Something else has been happening to which we have paid little attention: there was a time when death was familiar in every household. People were dying all the time: children, young adults, older adults, old people, and they died at home. This happens only rarely nowadays. We hardly see it. People die in hospitals, away from home. And they die later in life. I have had patients who, at the age of forty or fifty, had never known what it was to have somebody close to them die. This is something new in human life. Death has lost some of its imminent and urgent reality. It too has become a kind of abstraction. It is often inaccurate for us to think that a patient who, for any reason, contemplates an act that might be self-destructive, has a really immanent and realistic sense of what this means, that he pictures himself as no longer existing. Very frequently they do not.

On the other hand, we see movies and TV showing death; but not my own death or the death of somebody close to me. It is, rather, the death of somebody up on the screen. It is introduced into the home until there is a curious dichotomy in the whole growing-up process, from childhood on. We do not yet know what this means. Do all levels of awareness and of unawareness, do the symbolic and the realistic meaning of dying mean the same? It all happens at a distance; it cannot happen to me. Youngsters go into wars with a deep conviction that it could happen to any other fellow, not to them. This is not anything new or strange, but of course it makes the problem that much more complicated. As we face and try to study this extraordinarily subtle and complicated problem we need to accept its subtlety and its complications.

A few examples: a high-spirited, healthy, energetic, resilient youngster faces a very serious and incapacitating illness. He cannot tolerate the idea of living without the verve, the physical energy, and intellectual energy that he has always had. So he tries to delay his illness. How does he do it? By skipping his insulin, by pretending that he is not sick. If you do not take insulin, then it is not true that you are sick. He may end up dead. Is he trying to commit suicide? But to lump this behavior all under big gross generalizations—masochism, sadism, suicide—is to do violence to the facts.

Another example: Quadriplegia, which can be produced in a variety of different ways, may affect different lives in essentially the same way, but the process by which the disease was developed can be very different. It follows that the preventive process is going to have to be different, and the early recognition of it is going to take different skills. The same thing can be said of fever, of dehydration, of anemia, and of course the same thing is true of all psychological symptoms. No matter how one acquires a height phobia, it is going to have some similar effects on his life—unless he happens to live where there are no high buildings or high trees or high mountains. The effect on the living is going to be the same, but the way by which he developed his illness, the process of illness, is going to be different. We psychiatrists, psychoanalysts, biochemists, neurobiochemists, clinical psychologists, sociologists, geneticists, and statisticians have all stopped thinking about this. We act as though it were all one illness, simply because it ends with a certain symptom and the symptom has certain consequences, forgetting how important the differences are in the paths by which the symptoms are produced.

The key is in the concept of multiple determinants of human health and illness. There are many ways to climb the mountain. And whenever the feedback from the final symptom is the same, and particularly if it is as dramatic as it is when suicide results, we are most likely to forget the complexity and the diversity of the process of illnesses with which we are dealing.

I have known patients who injured themselves, sometimes very seriously and sometimes fatally although not immediately, in a kind of trancelike state, a kind of hysterical trance. It is a very different kind of a suicide from the one that happens in a state of rage or a state of acute depression or in a state of panic. I recall a woman of extraordinary strength who was able to stand up to strains that most of us would not be able to take, had never known what it is to experience an anxiety state. One day something touched off an explosion of anxiety and she jumped out the window. But she did not die. That was how I was able to know anything about it. Now this again is a totally different kind of experience. And again, it showed how different the processes can be.

And then there is the patient who makes a gesture that is self-destructive. In one instance it was a woman who was involved in multiple automobile accidents for a very interesting and special reason. She wanted to go back to the beginning, it was a kind of brinkmanship of the beginning of life, but never over the brink, so that she could start and live life all over again.

On the Nature of Suicide

Obviously, we cannot lump any one example in with all the other methods, all the other purposes, or all the other goals. These are different processes even though the ultimate result seems to be the same. All these raise issues that we cannot shut our eyes to if we are going to face up to the extraordinary complexity of the problems that we are dealing with in the area of human self-destruction.

8

Discussion

A Question
of Research

ᘓᘓᘓᘓᘓᘓᘓᘓᘓᘓᘓᘓᘓᘓᘓᘓ

STENGEL: I like to refer to Dr. Choron's remarks about the ideas of death that people have. He asks:
Do those who commit suicide have a different concept of
death? This is a very important question. I think that if one
speaks in terms of concepts of death, one must consider the
difference between what a normal death does to other people
and what a suicidal death does to other people. I think that
the study of natural death, and the concepts derived from

them, will not help us a great deal in the study of suicide, because suicide is not natural death; it is a self-inflicted death, inflicted on ourselves and on others, and many of the effects of death on others do not apply to suicidal deaths.

CHORON: I do not think that the attitudes of a suicidal person and his notions of death are a decisive factor. It is just one of the many factors that have, until now, been neglected and should be taken into consideration. I also pointed out that for a therapist who deals with a potentially suicidal patient or who is occupied with the process of his rehabilitation, talking about the notions of death may help to reestablish communication between the patient and the therapist. It may also have diagnostic value in the sense that it may help us, even if not decisively, to establish the lethality of the patient.

As far as the different effect of a natural death or a suicidal death on others is concerned, I am in full agreement with Dr. Stengel. There is another aspect to this whole death situation. I think that not sufficient attention has been paid to the difference between the death of another person, even of a loved one, and what I would call my own death. My death is something entirely different from the death of another person. It is possibly so different that we might even agree with the suggestion of Percy Bridgman, the famous physicist who committed suicide when he was in his eighties—that we should try to think of a different term when we talk about "my death" than about death in general terms.

We all have certain notions of what death means. These notions—whether they are things which we have been told about or ideas we have constructed out of our religious education or our reading—somehow have to go through extraordinary changes when they really become acute. In other words, someone who has been brought up in the belief of immortality or resurrection or salvation can go along with it as long as he is in good health, but when the critical moment comes and he realizes that his own days are counted, there might be a very important change; the same, of course, applies to a suicidal person. A person may entertain certain notions about death, and then something might happen to him where he, for some reason or other, thinks that the only solution is to end it all. And then, of course, this end presents itself in a different way. He might develop fantasies about death which he did not entertain in health or when he thought that death was still quite removed.

We also do not realize enough that we all live with this extraordinary illusion without which we possibly might not be able to live at all—namely, that our own death is practically impossible. After Freud, Schilder made his very interesting investigation, the first study of attitudes of normal people and neurotics toward death and dying in which he came to the conclusion that death is unavoidable but incredible; that no one really believes in his own death.

What is going on in the mind of a suicidal person? We know from many studies that many suicidal people do not really think that they will be dead when they kill themselves. Therefore, I think that in this connection between suicide and death, the differences in attitudes toward death before the suicidal intent and during the suicidal intent are quite an important factor and should be considered.

KUBIE: I think it is very dangerous for us to present our speculations about these issues and it is rather striking that it has been very difficult to get really factual data about them. There are many areas where factual data could be secured; for instance, what about the incidence of suicide of troops who have been in actual combat when the reality of mutilation or death had been brought very close to them, in contradistinction to the remoteness of actual experience of death in the lives of most human beings in our present culture. There are many other places where this could be studied. During World War II, I spent a great deal of time in Canada for the Director General of Medical Services of the Canadian army. In the course of that time I saw a great deal of Canadian soldiers from small isolated French-Canadian villages where medical care at that time was at a very low ebb, where the incidence of infant mortality, early childhood mortality, maternal mortality were all very high. Those youngsters were probably the most hypochondriacal neurotic young people I had ever, as a group, had dealings with, but suicide almost never occurred.

Whether this preoccupation with the fantasy of death-dealing sickness in some way dealt with and eliminated the need to do away with themselves or whether the direct confrontation with death in the family and in the villages all around them made it a close reality which had some influence on the fate of their impulses, I do not know. The impulse, the potentiality, is there in everyone. These are issues that have to be studied and not speculated about. The observations are striking, but I do not think we use them enough or explore them closely enough to know how they relate to the actual execution of the impulse.

CHORON: I would agree with Dr. Kubie that the main difficulty is an investigation of the phenomena which we have discussed. Maybe in the future somebody will come up with some new ideas or new approaches to this problem so that we can move beyond conjectures, insights, and speculations and put our thoughts on a scientific basis.

A last remark I would like to make also has something to do with Freud's theories of death instinct and his famous statement that the unconscious does not know its own death, which has been accepted on faith by most psychologists, by most students of suicide, and, of course, by most psychoanalysts. I do not think that the fact that the unconscious does not know its own death, or does not know of death at all, is really something we have to accept on faith. I think this is an area in which some probing and some thinking have to be done.

On the other hand, why should it be so surprising that the unconscious which, by definition, is not supposed to know anything at all, does not know of death? And even if the unconscious does not know of death, what does that prove? After all, we are most of the time conscious people and we know of death precisely because we have consciousness and self-awareness, and, of course, the death awareness is the result of self-awareness. So, I think this is also one of the very urgent problems to be investigated. Such research might help us to understand not only our ideas about death and our attitudes toward death but also some of the aspects of the problems of suicide.

SHNEIDMAN: What is the role of subintentioned deaths? Do we not miss too much if we count data only under the rubric of suicide? Do we now not have to extend our concepts and think not only of intentioned deaths and what those acts were intended to achieve, but also of other categories such as subintentional deaths?

STENGEL: It all depends on how you define *subintention*. The large majority of people who perform suicidal attempts, and many of those who commit suicide, do not do these with the idea of ending their lives, but with a feeling, I don't care whether I live or die. This is what I had in mind when I said that most people who commit suicidal acts do not either want to live or to die, but they want to do both at the same time.

If this comes under the definition of subintentioned death, then, of course, this is a very common thing, if such a suicide ends in death. On the other hand, if Dr. Shneidman has in mind patterns of behavior which Dr. Menninger has described so brilliantly, which are manifestations of these damaging tendencies or self-destructive tendencies, without any, however vague, suicidal intention, then, of course, this widens the concept enormously. At any rate, it is very important that we know at any given time what we are talking about. One can include those patterns, but then, of course, suicide becomes an almost unlimited area of behavior patterns.

MENNINGER: I want to acknowledge Dr. Stengel's great contribution to my own thinking when he emphasized the fact that the suicidal attempt could be, not as we had always thought, an evidence of despair, but an evidence of hope—an evidence of the hope that someone will be found who will recognize how much they can help the person in distress. This seems like merely playing with words, but actually it inverts the emphasis because we really used tacitly to take it for granted that the despair was in some way justified, that a person's life is rather terrible and perhaps we do not know how much he suffered, so it overwhelmed him. This new thought looks at it in a different way. Not that suicide is a logical outcome of depression, but rather that suicide is the evidence of depression that has not succeeded in accomplishing its mission. The mission of a depression is to get revenge. Depression is to hurt somebody else, not ourselves. By being depressed, by putting on a big pout as it were, we can show somebody how much they have hurt us, therefore, how much we may hurt them. Forty years ago we used to think that the logical outcome of this is that the depressed person is going to be pretty overwhelmed and that he will make suicidal attempts, and therefore we must take certain measures to allay the depression.

Today, I think we should take certain measures to allay not the depression but to redirect the depression, specifically from its exhibitionistic, self-punitive, and masochistic forms, but also from this clinical form into some nonclinical form. I think that is the current idea of treatment in psychiatry. If we are not going to treat symptoms—the old way of pity—then how shall we treat them? How should we react to the message that they convey? What does one do when there is a cry for help? Would you give help? What do you do when there is an urge to pout? You have to overcome the pouting, for the pouting has a meaning—and so on.

DUBLIN: I would like to focus a little more attention on the administrative aspect of the working of our suicide prevention centers, specifically on the difference that has developed in the administrative operations in our centers as contrasted with those, let us say, in Britain, under the guidance of Reverend Chad Varah, Dr. Stengel, and the Samaritans all over England, Scotland, and Wales.

To be more specific: according to what I saw there and what I have read in Varah's account[1] and in my conversations with Stengel, the lay volunteer is not satisfied with a telephone contact. He goes far beyond that in a great many cases. He is also a visitor, a befriender. He establishes a living contact with his client, which may go on for a long time until he is satisfied that his friend has been reestablished, whether it be in his job or whether the situation with his wife has been corrected, or whatever it was that brought this individual to the point of despair and to the attention of the Samaritan office.

There does not seem to be any great fear of doing mischief or of overreaching the mark. I understand that to be what Varah would call a distinguishing feature of that operation—which has captured the attention of that large country.

That is not true in this country. We are developing another pattern and I confess that I am fearful that we are not utilizing all of the facilities we have; that we are overcareful; that we have been overwhelmed with the authority of the professionals who have stood in the way of the work of our volunteers. They have stood in the way even of the choice of volunteers. I have listened to one of those who has been

93

most active in writing the manual of rules for the choosing of the volunteers and I confess I have been dismayed. If you are going to run a suicide prevention center you will need volunteers. This country is full of capable people of good will, just as Britain is, and we should not be afraid to make mistakes and to learn. And we will not make many mistakes. I was tremendously interested in the work I have heard of in this country where the volunteers were picked from the community by those who were directing the center, and then trained—and they had the right to fall out of the picture if they did not feel at home—and then tested, and the incompetents, the unprepared, the inept, and the dangerous plucked out. There was no fear there. There was rather an attitude of accepting the community's facilities and then going on from there.

I have in mind more than that. As an experienced public health man, I have in mind that we have a tremendous resource that we have not used at all. I have in mind the public health nurse who is just barely getting in on the scene as I watch the procession here. We have scarcely brought her into the picture. There are thousands of public health nurses whose careers have made the public health movement a reality. We have never realized what we owe to those women. In this new development we should not be afraid to use their skills. These are competent and able women. They know how to handle people. Working hand in glove with volunteers, what an aid that would be to overcome inertia and many fears.

I bring this to your attention because I think we are at the crossroads. We are going to have to solve this problem. We shall have to put content into our service. It cannot be left to the telephone and to a referral. Those are not enough. You have to establish a human relationship. It has been done in Britain and they have succeeded brilliantly.

I want to have Dr. Stengel, who knows this situation as no one else and who also knows our American situation, comment on this issue.

STENGEL: There is a considerable difference, I admit. It has been said about the British that they have a tremendous faith in the well-meaning amateur, and, of course, it has been said about the Americans that they have a tremendous faith in professionalism. This British faith in amateurs and even suspicion of the expert has been praised, but has always been blamed for a good deal of the trouble that British industry and the country as a whole is finding itself in.

There are certain differences in outlook between these two societies, and although the British approach does appeal to many and it seems to mobilize a great deal of the latent help within society, possibly it may not, in the long run, prove as effective.

Dr. Dublin refers to the function of the Samaritans, which they call "befriending." It is quite right that they say that the telephone contact is only an emergency service and that the real purpose of their service is befriending. This is what they are trying to do. At the same time, I must say I have often addressed Samaritans and I have been particularly interested in that aspect of their work. While it is only a beginning, it is a very complex and at times rather tricky and dangerous activity for people who are not adequately equipped and skilled in handling human relations. But they persist with this, quite rightly, and it is thus one of the functions of the courses they have from doctors and sociologists—to improve their knowledge and skill in this particular area.

I refer to something that Dr. Havighurst said about social class. There is, of course, still in most parts of the world, an overrepresentation in suicide statistics of the upper social classes. Why this should not have been found in this country, recently, it is difficult to know. Possibly American society is

95

perhaps nearer to the classless society than Americans themselves realize. But, anyway, all this depends very much on the reliability of the statistics. As Dr. Havighurst has referred to statistics a great deal, may I tell you that one of the features of recent suicide research has been that it has had no respect for sacred cows, and statistics, including suicide rates, is one of the sacred cows we recently have treated with some disrespect. Norman Farberow and I have made a study of the methods of registration of suicide all over the world and we have come to the conclusion that suicide rates in various countries, and often in the same country, are simply not comparable. I have suggested that only those suicide rates should be compared whose direct comparability has been proved. This means that a good deal of the national statistics that World Health Organization proudly presents every year should be taken with many grains of salt and there are certain myths about them that deserve to be exploded.

HAVIGHURST: I am also concerned about this matter of the reliability of the statistics. Let me cite a particular case. Take that difference between Norway and Denmark, which puzzles everybody. Over the years, Denmark has a suicide rate of about twice that of Norway. Do you think this is due to some differences in the way the statistics are collected or interpreted?

STENGEL: I think that the Danish suicide rate is high, but I do not know whether it is higher than that of the United States. The United States has a suicide rate of about 11, just like Britain—this is the official suicide rate. I should not be at all surprised if, in fact, the incidence of suicide in this country and in Britain was higher than that of Denmark and Sweden. This is what I mean when I say only comparable data should be compared. You cannot compare the Danish and Swedish suicide rates with the British and American rates. The British and American suicide rate is based on coroner's verdicts, and coroner's verdicts are based on criteria of the criminal court. Unless you have positive evidence, through a suicide note or through some communication by a witness who comes forward, the coroner cannot give a suicide verdict. He insists upon positive evidence. In Los Angeles, when we discussed this, we were told about the study by Theodore Curphey undertaken with a large group of American coroners in a number of cities and it turned out that their suicide rates were not at all comparable with each other.

If you divide deaths through poisoning into suicidal deaths, indeterminate deaths, and accidental deaths, you would expect, in the same country, to find an approximately similar relationship. But this was not what Dr. Curphey found. The discrepancies among those groups were absolutely fantastic when some forty coroner's records were compared.

It was also interesting that when psychologists and psychiatrists were called in, as occurred in Los Angeles, the proportion of accidental and indeterminate deaths suddenly dropped to a fraction. This shows that suicide rates are not comparable. In Denmark and Sweden there are no coroners. There are medical experts, forensic experts, who decide the cause of death. Therefore these cannot be compared. The same applies to Austria.

HAVIGHURST: Would you mind my pressing this a little bit? It would seem to me that the methods of determining mode of death and of signing death certificates would not be very different between Norway and Denmark. Would that not be right?

STENGEL: One would expect higher suicide rates in Denmark. Denmark is a densely populated country, while Norway is a very thinly distributed population. But this was discussed also, and it was pointed out that there was an inverse relationship between accidental deaths through drowning and suicidal deaths. Now, in Norway, the proportion of accidental deaths through drowning is fantastic compared with Denmark. So while I would expect Norway, in view of the largely rural composition of the population, to have a lower suicide rate, I certainly do not think the difference is as great as it is made out or as it appears in statistics. This is the reason why I also find Herbert Hendin's study, *Suicide and Scandinavia,*[2] which is based on this enormous difference of suicide rate, quite unconvincing.

SHNEIDMAN: Dr. Dublin, do you want to comment on the issue of statistics? Certainly your name is closely identified with this whole area.

DUBLIN: Dr. Shneidman reminds me that I carry a statistician's hat, among other hats, and that I should perhaps close this discussion on statistics. That I will not do, for there is too much fun involved in listening to these uncertainties that we are all confronted with. One thing is fairly certain. Large numbers of suicides—that is true not only here but in all countries—are not reported. So that in looking at these figures we would be well advised to look at long trends to see the way things are going and not be overwhelmed with changes from year to year, and in comparing figures from country to country.

Points made by Dr. Stengel are well taken. If you look carefully you will find the explanations. They are not always on the surface but they are there to account for differences which are hard to understand. I, too, was concerned in my treatment of the situation abroad in my book, *Suicide,*[3] and I called attention to the differences among the three Scandinavian countries. Dr. Stengel knows better than I just why the figures for Norway are so unreasonably low. They are not accurate.

I am more concerned with the attempt to use statistical methods in evaluating the work that we are going to do in our own prevention centers. It is, of course, a most important part of the operation to know where we are going and what is coming out of all this effort. But we must not be overwhelmed by rough calculations showing a drop in the local death rate and then ascribe it to the operation of a center. That is asking for too much, because next year's rate might be 10 per cent higher due to your more careful certification of deaths or to the greater interest that your own work is bringing about. So there is work for the statistician and scientist in evaluating the suicidal situation, both from point of view of the completed suicides and point of view of the preventive effort. A good deal has to be done in the way of perfecting the original material; much has to be done to make the records in the prevention centers adequate so that at the end of the year we know something about where the clients are and what is happening to them, whether they are alive, or if dead, what they died of, and so on, so that all this information will be reflected in the statistics. I would say that there is plenty to be done, but do not draw conclusions with regard to the effectiveness of your work on the score of whether the number of suicides in the community goes up or down. You would do well to wait.

References

[1] Chad Varah, *The Samaritans* (New York: Macmillan, 1966).

[2] Herbert Hendin, *Suicide and Scandinavia* (New York: Grune and Stratton, 1964).

[3] Louis I. Dublin, *Suicide: A Sociological and Statistical Study* (New York: Ronald Press, 1964).

TWO

SUICIDE AND THE WILL

9

The Phenomenology of Suicide

Leslie H. Farber

~~~~~~~~~~~~~~~~~~~~~~~

In Dostoyevsky's novel *The Possessed*, there is a character named Kierlov who commits suicide. A particularly telling passage reads as follows:

> *Man has done nothing but invest God so as to go on living and not kill himself. I can't understand how an*

*atheist can know there is no God and not kill himself
on the spot. To recognize that there is no God and
not to recognize at the same instant that one is God,
one's self is an absurdity, else one would certainly kill
themselves. If you recognize it you are solvent and
then you won't kill yourself but will live in the greatest
glory and immortality. But, one, the first must kill
themselves or else will begin and prove it. So I certainly must kill myself to begin and prove it. Now I
am only a God against my will and I am unhappy
because I am bound to assert my will. All are unhappy
because all are afraid to express their will. Man has
heights to be so unhappy and so poor because he has
been afraid to assert his will in the highest point, and
has shown his self will only in little things, like a
schoolboy.*[1]

Because most of this chapter is about the nature of
willing in regard to suicide, it is important at the beginning
to make a sharp distinction between the act of suicide and
what I call the life of suicide, that is, thinking about suicide.

Gabriel Marcel has written: "The fact that suicide is
always possible is the essential starting point of any genuine
metaphysical thought."[2] As a companion notion, one could
mention that once Nietzsche wrote: "The thought of suicide
is a strong consolation; one can get through many a bad night
with it."[3] In effect, Nietzsche is saying the same thing as
Marcel. The thought of suicide allows him to challenge his
own life metaphysically. It might equally be said that the
possibilities of suicide will always oppose psychiatry's efforts to
rid itself of metaphysical concern, for once that possibility dis-
rupts the civilized and ordinary boundaries of psychotherapy,
every technical category loses its ordinary place in our thinking and must be questioned with a new urgency, or else ex-
ploited in a manner which robs it of whatever truthful meaning it may have earned.

Martin Buber stated: "The act of suicide, it is a trap

door which suddenly springs open."⁴ What else can one say? To judge from the psychiatric literature, one can say a great deal.

It is my impression that, to the man who kills himself, the act of suicide may be a trap door suddenly sprung. To the psychoanalyst it seems rather to resemble a psychological staircase, leading step by step to an inescapable culmination. Whether the staircase goes up or down, it must always be traveled backwards; that is, confronted with the fact of suicide, the analyst must construct his explanation in reverse, laying motive upon motive and strategy upon strategy until he reaches some finality. Having arrived at the end of the staircase he may then retrace the steps forward, issuing those prescriptions for preventing the act.

I would suggest that this staircase and trap door exist principally in the psychoanalyst's head, rather than in the real world. On the other hand, the world is full of trap doors, even though the only ones we can be sure of are those that have already been sprung. A trap door offers very little to an individual bent on expiration. It is my suspicion that the staircase model leads us not to greater understanding but rather away from the issue. It prevents us, right at the outset, from considering the possibility that the act of suicide is not the final move in a chain of causation; that perhaps it is not caused at all in a psychological sense.

I believe that there is a more fruitful approach: to leave aside, for the moment, the suicidal act itself and to contemplate the life of suicide, which must be seen not as a situation or state of mind which leads to the act, but, whether the act eventually occurs or not, as a life of its own. Between the act and the life of suicide there exists a difference, not of degree but of quality, that is as profound as that between dreaming and telling about a dream.

Buber would describe dreaming as that state which

105

precedes the split into the psychological and the physical, and we would agree that waking up confers on dreams a reputation that they do not deserve. Dreaming, according to Buber, is nonphenomenal, unlike our waking state, and, therefore, always opposes our attempts to capture or expose it existentially, inasmuch as such attempts belong to the split between the psychological and physical.[5]

Something similar may be said of suicide. Those who make suicidal plans and those who try to frustrate those plans (either for understanding or intervention) share the dilemma of insisting on knowing the unknowable. For the victim, the act puts an end to his efforts to penetrate the state itself; and for the investigator, like the dream researcher, the fact is that he knows that the moment he intervenes in a suicidal attempt, he is no longer the privileged individual to the state itself.

There are times when we may converse with a dreamer, just as there are times when we may talk to the man perched on the ledge of a tall building. In the former instance we talk from different worlds. He must awake to mine or I must sleep to his. In the case of suicide I may prevent him without getting any closer to the typography of the act itself or he may repudiate me by jumping, in which case he relinquishes his advantage as a psychological audience to become total action as he falls through the trap door, and even if he accidentally survives his fall for both himself and his questioner, he stands once again outside the state that both wished to penetrate.

I have labored this distinction between the act of suicide and the life of suicide because when we come to examine the issue in terms of will, we find we must make a similar distinction between two kinds of willing.

Kierkegaard in describing despair as a sickness unto death said it is a state in which we long to die and cannot. I would like to elaborate on that statement because I think it pertains to anyone anticipating or planning the possibility of suicide. On the one hand he longs to die (or he wills to die); on the other hand he cannot, meaning that there is something within him, which can also be called will, that refuses the suicidal attempt.

Two kinds of willing are involved: The person planning suicide, thinking about arranging his affairs and about the effects his act is going to have on his friends and family, is engaged in what I would call conscious willing, because he is aware of the place of will in the plans and plots that he devises. He is even aware of his efforts. On the other hand, he is forever being reminded almost in the mid-state of suicidal plots that his life is still going on; after he has had a meal, he says to himself, What am I doing, eating now, when I have already decided to die? It doesn't make any sense.

But each of those observations about life itself as an ongoing thing is grasped almost after the fact. He can say to himself, Because I am going to die there is no point in feeding myself. In that instance his conscious will to do takes priority over something that is more unacknowledged about staying alive.

I propose that the will to kill oneself and the will to stay alive are of quite different orders. The will to stay alive, if there is such a will, merely states that one wills to pursue one's existence, come what may. There is no concrete object for the will of staying alive. It is unlike the discrete, specific, and concrete act of killing oneself. One decides merely to pursue one's life, but the pursuit of one's life is forever offering evidence of that pursuit without revealing the specific place of will.

Let me use another example. My wife and I have quite different ways of entering the cold water of a lake. She simply runs into the water and starts swimming. I am forever holding back with my fear of cold water and my conscious will, so to speak, so that I proceed rather gingerly to test the water with one foot, and then I will force myself to move a little more, the idea being that I am going to become accustomed to the cold water, but always I reach a point where there is nothing to do but dive in. The diving in is what I would call the first realm of will in which will itself is unconscious; that is, after the event, after I have dived into the water, I may say, I dived into the water because I willed myself to dive into the water, but at the moment of diving I was not aware of the place of will as I was in the first instance where I very gingerly went through various stages, always consciously willing one stage after another until I came to the final necessity of diving in. Although this analogy is a rather trival one it nonetheless corresponds in a way to the person who wills not to die at the same time that he wills to kill himself.

   A few words about the place of this conscious will and the willing to die: such a person, I have to assume, is undergoing the questioning of his entire existence. His whole life has been put into question: who is he, where is he, what has he been about all these years, what acts of betrayal has he committed, either actively or by omission, and so on. With that sort of estrangement or despair, he tends to fall back more and more on this same conscious will in order to transcend the estrangement. If he finds it hard to be with others and to start any ordinary conversation, in effect he wills himself to look interested, to talk, and to look attentive. All these particular aspects of life are, of course, beyond such conscious willing. One cannot will attention. One either listens or he does not listen, he responds or he does not respond. So, the consequence of such willing is a state of what I would call willlessness. Whatever venture appears to him as a proper object for his will, he is quickly visited by a sense of futility and that can proceed even to putting on his clothes; it certainly pertains to meeting with a group of people.

As his own conscious will, in a sense, becomes more isolated from his other faculties, such as imagination, foresight, judgment, humor, and so on, as he becomes more willful toward his existence, he experiences himself as more willless. It is at this point that the issue of suicide exercises a demonic fascination, because to all the questions about his own being, where he has been, where he is going to go, whether this is the right life, and so on, suicide offers an answer. If he accuses himself of being timid, then courage is contained within the act of suicide. If he accuses himself of being dishonest in his connection with his fellows, then suicide offers an opportunity for at last going through with what he has already promised himself, or promised other people. If he accuses himself of being unable to bear the pain of existence, then suicide offers a confirmation of his bravery.

If you ask such a person, How do you know your life is unbearable, he answers you that it has to be unbearable, otherwise he would not be thinking of suicide. So, in effect, he may go through the act and kill himself in order to prove that life is unbearable.

You will note that I talk about a kind of willing toward existence in which the role of will itself is unconscious, although it can be talked about *after* the event. In one way, this sort of willing might be seen as some sort of anthropological principle of life, that is, the will to persevere, come what may.

The hideous question so far as this topic is concerned is what occurs that allows this conscious willing toward death to overcome this first realm, willing to persevere. These two kinds of willing are naturally interrelated, each contributing to the other. How is it that the imagination of the potential sui-

109

cide eventually so diminishes this intention to preserve life that the person goes through with the act?

I have already stated that I regard the act itself as a trap door—and yet I would be interested in speculation about the issue. It does seem to me that in this age of drugs we are offered a double difficulty because the sort of wholeness for which a man yearns in the act of suicide and with which he is consciously plotting suicide is offered by the very drug with which he hopes to end his life, so that often one gets a double phenomenon: that is, the person takes drugs in order to get the courage to experience the wholeness with which to end his life. It seems to me that this is becoming a more and more common occurrence.

References

[1] Fyodor Dostoyevsky, *The Possessed* (New York: New American Library, 1962).
[2] Gabriel Marcel, *The Philosophy of Existentialism* (New York: Citadel Press, 1961).
[3] Friedrich Nietzsche, *Beyond Good and Evil* (Chicago: Regnery, 1965).
[4] Martin Buber, Personal communication.
[5] Martin Buber, Public lecture, 1958.

10

Jack D. Douglas

The Absurd
in Suicide

ᘁᘁᘁᘁᘁᘁᘁᘁᘁᘁᘁᘁᘁᘁᘁᘁ

There are two general dimensions to the problem of determining the relations between the will and suicide: First, there is the problem of defining suicide; how should we define suicide and how is the will related to this definition? Second, there is the problem of determining empirically and analyzing theoretically in what ways willing (or intention) is involved in actual occurrences of suicidal behavior.

As most students of suicide are aware, there have

111

been dozens of definitions of suicide proposed over the last few hundred years in the Western world. As indicated in *The Social Meanings of Suicide*,[1] there seem to be at least six basic dimensions of meaning involved (to varying degrees and in different combinations) in these many definitions: (1) the *initiation* of an act that leads to the death of the initiator; (2) the *willing* of an act that leads to the death of the willer; (3) the willing of self-destruction; (4) the loss of will; (5) the *motivation* to be dead (or to die) which leads to the initiation of an act that leads to the death of the initiator; and (6) the *knowledge* of an actor that actions that he initiates tend to produce the objective state of death.

The confusing profusion of formal definitions of suicide is probably due primarily to the attempt by students of suicide to define suicide in the abstract. Inasmuch as almost all of these students tacitly accepted the positivistic tradition of scientific thought, which involves a profound distrust of common-sense thinking, they almost universally assume that the scientist must define his categories quite independently of the common-sense meanings of the category. As Durkheim, the foremost sociological representative of this tradition of thought, put it: ". . . the scholar cannot take as the subject of his research roughly assembled groups of facts corresponding to words of common usage."[2]

However, when we look at how these scientific students of suicide have actually gone about defining suicide, we find something quite different. With hardly an exception, they have actually constructed their formal definitions out of parts of the common-sense meanings of suicide. Each theorist has simply emphasized those parts that fit his own theoretical preconceptions and arbitrarily excluded from consideration those that did not. In the case of those scientists who, like Durkheim, relied upon official information on suicide, such as the official statistics, there is no question that they were in fact indirectly relying upon the common-sense meanings of suicide, regardless of their contempt for common-sense definition. The officials responsible for categorizing suicide as the cause of death—the doctors, police, coroners (who are often not doctors), medical examiners, and various public health officials—are themselves relying entirely upon their common-sense conceptions of suicide to decide whether a given death is a suicide.[3] In a current study of county coroners and medical examiners not one was found who was relying upon any formal or official definition of suicide.[4] A few pathologists made reference to a well-known text on forensic medicine but they did not know whether the text contained a formal definition of suicide. In fact, almost all of these officials seem surprised by the question concerning whether they use an official or formal definition of suicide. As far as can be judged, they take it for granted that anyone doing his job would simply know the meaning of suicide— necessarily, the common-sense meaning. In addition, psychiatrists working with suicidal patients are, in almost all cases, actually working with the common-sense definition of suicide, since these cases are generally defined for them by other persons, frequently the patients themselves, as suicidal. (Psychiatrists generally do ask whether each case really will do it, but this is very different from asking whether a given communication is suicidal.)

This ultimate use of the common-sense meanings as the basis for the scientific analysis should not be surprising. After all, these scientists were fundamentally concerned with understanding and explaining what members of our society (common-sensically) see to be suicide. Since these everyday phenomena are what they are most concerned with understanding and since the vast majority of them today would agree that individuals commit actions because of certain meanings these actions have for them, there is every reason why they should be fundamentally concerned with the common-sense meanings of suicide. The problem has been that they have attempted to impose their abstract definitions on the common-sense term, and this imposition has resulted in confusion. What they need to do—and what has been attempted in *The Social Meanings of Suicide*[5]—is determine what the members of society mean by suicide and what there is in the meanings of suicide to them that leads them to commit or not to commit suicide.

When we do study the common-sense meanings of suicide, we find that it has the various meanings already presented. It seems reasonably clear that the existence of these different common-sense meanings makes the very meaning of suicide problematic for the members of society and helps to cause the disagreements over whether a given death is a "suicide"—that is, in some instances people certainly are not hiding the fact of suicide, but sincerely give a different meaning to the term *suicide*, which leads them to believe that a given instance is not a suicide. While these conflicts in the meaning of suicide are important for various reasons, it is true that one common-sense meaning is far more frequently found than the others: that is, the intention to kill oneself. As soon as the intention to die by one's own action is extended to cover "or by any action more indirect," then people become much more uncertain about whether a death is a suicide and the disagreements become more acute.

Insofar as will and intention mean roughly the same thing today,[6] this naturalistic approach to the definition of suicide would lead us to conclude that willing (or intending) to die by one's own action is the most common, hence most important, meaning of suicide in Western societies.

Even if we accept this naturalistic definition of suicide, it is by no means obvious how this meaning of suicide would be important in explaining suicidal actions. That members of our society consider or believe suicide to be intentional or willed by the very term they use to refer to the act does not make it true. It could in fact be the case that there are no events to which the term could correctly be applied. The question of the relation between intention and suicide in this respect is certainly an empirical question.

I believe there are two important general relations between intention and committing an act that is socially categorized as suicide.

In the early part of the nineteenth century it was frequently argued that suicide was so irrational that people committing the act must be insane and incapable of willing anything. With the advent of the dominance of Freudian thinking in psychiatry in this century this irrationalist theory of suicide was carried one step further. The most basic idea of this approach is that there are unconscious forces lying behind and determining the conscious ideas, intentions, willings, and actions of individuals. This approach (a) assumes that the abstract theory (whether Freudian, Adlerian, Jungian, or whatever) is valid and applicable to any new case; (b) observes the individual case; and (c) interprets this case in specific terms of the abstract theory (thereby allowing the individual facts observed to have some effect) in such a way that what is observed is always taken to represent unobservable, unconscious, or irrational forces.

I suspect that in Western society this approach can have some therapeutic benefit for patients (that is, it makes them feel better), simply because the psychoanalytic process involves an intensive *training* of the patient in a whole ideological world-view directed toward health. Those patients who trust in the "scientific" and curative effect of this relation and can, therefore, accept the whole world-view rather than showing "irrational (for example, Oedipal) resistance" to it, come to see their lives in its terms, proudly adopt the Freudian and psychiatric language, and "feel better." While far more people are "cured" in exactly the same way by Christian conversion, such a "scientific" therapy, which clothes magical thought in the garb and prestige of materialistic science, is probably necessary in our transitional period when most of us are half-religious and half-scientific.

But we should not allow these therapeutic goals of psychiatry to blind us to what I believe are reasonably clear truths. First of all, it should be apparent that by any accepted criteria of scientific truth these depth-psychological approaches are not at all scientific. For them, the "real" truth is known before the new case is approached and this "real" truth is always unobservable. I propose that, instead of assuming that each new observation will be irrelevant, we take the immediately observable phenomena as being "real" in themselves and of fundamental importance in understanding and explaining why individuals commit such actions as suicide. By this case study approach one would concentrate on getting very careful observations and descriptions of as many cases as possible. Since all of the many etiological studies of committed and attempted suicide have uncovered very few, if any, consistent relations between childhood experiences and suicidal actions years later, it has become increasingly apparent that the situational events, meanings and actions are of crucial importance in determining whether suicidal actions are committed. As most people involved with suicidal individuals realize, life and death generally hinge on the immediate situation and often on events which to the uninvolved observer would appear to be relatively inconsequential. For this reason, the situational events should be observed and recorded in as much microscopic detail as possible. The theorist can then compare such careful descriptive case studies to determine the common elements and processes involved, especially the meanings of such actions to the individuals involved.

My previous analyses of this sort have led me to conclude that the individuals attempting and committing suicide in the great majority of cases are certainly very conscious of what they are doing, intend to commit the acts (though we know that any "intention to die" is almost always ambivalent), are very concerned about the specific meanings they and others give to the acts, and do act "rationally" to construct just those meanings for their actions which they want others to accept. The thoughts and actions of such people may not appear rational or logical to an uninvolved observer, who generally assumes that anything leading to death could only be chosen irrationally; and certainly there is very often a form of what Shneidman calls "catalogic" involved in their thinking, by which is meant that they implicitly assume that they will be alive after death.[7] But there is a cultural logic or rationality to this which materialistic scientists generally fail to see because they do not share the common religious and magical beliefs of most members of our society.

There are, of course, instances in which individuals commit suicidal actions in a fugue state[8] or against their will in a state of possession. There are even more cases in which individuals in confused states die by their own actions, but then these deaths are not normally considered suicides by the members of our society. However, the great majority of suicidal actions do involve rational intention; and these are the ones with which we are most concerned.

We must not conclude from this argument that all individuals who commit actions considered to be suicidal by members of our society intend to die. On the contrary, there are many cases of dangerous actions intentionally committed by individuals against themselves in which they have had no clear intention of dying; and there are even some cases in which individuals seem shocked to learn that they are dying, presumably because they have acted in a blind rage. In the vast majority of cases, however, individuals committing dangerous acts against themselves do have what they themselves see as some degree of intention to die. (Those that do not seem to have this intention are generally treated by members of our society as "not really being suicidal.") But there is also every indication that in the great majority of cases where there is such an intention to die, there is also an intention to use suicide, through the construction of certain meanings for others involved, so that they can live better, either in this world or the next. Suicide, then, is generally a highly ambivalent action. Even those individuals with very serious intentions of dying by suicide rarely give up hope of living. After taking pills, they call for help or move toward others; when cutting their throats they generally make "hesitation" cuts; and most individuals who attempt or commit suicide have given their friends and relatives serious warnings of their intentions to kill themselves.[9]

This high degree of ambivalence, with its consequent effects on behavior, is a major reason why there is such a large degree of existential absurdity involved in suicidal actions. But this unrationalizable gap between what the individuals intend and the outcomes of their actions is also caused by the independent action of the world—because members of our society, especially doctors and officials who are highly committed to preventing suicide or any death, intervene between the individuals' intended outcomes and the actual outcomes. Just at the outcomes are more likely to be death when the technical methods provided are more lethal, so are the outcomes more likely not to be death as medicine and its supporting agencies become more effective. An individual who commits a dangerous act against himself may die or he may live. Whether death actually occurs is only partially dependent on his intentions, plans, and actions. From his standpoint, then, whether he commits suicide, attempts suicide, or was not really trying to commit suicide is largely dependent on the irrational or absurd aspects of the human situation. He can try to control these, and may do so, but there is always an ultimate, irreducible element of absurdity.[10]

References

[1] Jack D. Douglas, *The Social Meanings of Suicide* (Princeton, N.J.: Princeton University Press, 1967), Appendix 2.

[2] Émile Durkheim, *Suicide* (New York: Free Press, 1951), p. 41.

[3] Douglas, *op. cit.*, Part III, "The Sociological Analysis of Social Meanings of Suicide," *Archives Européennes de Sociologie,* VII (1966), pp. 249–275, and "Suicide: The Social Element," *International Encyclopedia of the Social Sciences* (New York: Macmillan, 1968).

[4] This research project, "The Official Classification of Suicide as a Cause of Death," was supported by a grant from the National Institute of Health, Center for Studies of Suicide Prevention.

[5] See Douglas, *op. cit.*, Part IV. For a similar approach to analyzing the meanings of suicide, see Edwin S. Shneidman, "Sleep and Self-Destruction: A Phenomenological Approach," in E. S. Shneidman (Ed.), *Essays in Self-Destruction* (New York: Science House, 1967), pp. 510–539.

[6] Strictly speaking, even today will involves more the idea of *active* intending or deciding and committing oneself to a path of action than does intention.

[7] E. S. Shneidman, "The Logical, Psychological, and Ecological Environments of Suicide," *California Health, 17,* 1960, 193–196.

[8] See Douglas, *op. cit.*, Appendix 2.

[9] E. S. Shneidman and N. L. Farerow (Eds.), *Clues to Suicide* (New York: McGraw-Hill, 1957).

[10] I have analyzed suicide and the absurd in much greater detail in *Revenge Suicide,* Englewood Cliffs, New Jersey: Prentice-Hall (in press).

11

David Bakan

Suicide
and Immortality

In this paper I shall attempt to explicate a hypothetical psychological mechanism leading to suicide. The main idea can be stated rather simply: The person who commits suicide is one who, in reaction to the sense of his "being in question," to use Heidegger's expression, kills himself in order to place death under the control of the will. By placing death under the control of the will he opens up the possibility, in this paradoxical manner, of immortality; as though it were up to him whether he live or die; as though he chooses the time of death and could, had he so desired, not have died.

The pattern of the mechanism that I am trying to outline is hardly novel; it is a pattern that has been explicated quite richly, particularly in the writings of Alfred Adler. We are all aware of the student who, for example, "proves" to himself that he could perform well on an examination by not taking it. Willing his failure is evidence that had he so willed success he could have equally obtained it. One can multiply such examples. In the case of suicide the mechanism is applied to existence itself.

I have two embarrassments in connection with discussing suicide, and I discuss these embarrassments because they themselves appear to me to be probes into the nature of the phenomenon. My first embarrassment is that you should perhaps suspect that I myself might harbor some secret intention to commit suicide or that you might suspect that at some time in the past I have made an attempt to commit suicide. Indeed, my embarrassment appears to me to apply more generally than to myself alone when I peruse some of the professional literature on suicide and note the many ways by which writers on suicide equally announce to their audience that they consider the act of suicide something of which the weak or the sinful might be guilty, but of which there is no trace underneath their professional robes and roles.

I would take it that the very existence of the embarrassment strongly suggests that in some way the entertainment of the idea of suicide is evocative of some kind of original sin within each of us. I would identify the original sin as being simply the desire to live forever, wanting an immorality of flesh and blood, as Miguel de Unamuno, in his book, *The Tragic Sense of Life,* was frank enough to admit to for himself.

I once had occasion to see some correspondence be-

121

tween the superintendent of a mental hospital and a relative of a patient who had committed suicide in the hospital. The relative's letter was scathingly critical of the hospital, the staff, and the superintendent for allowing the suicide to take place. The superintendent's reply was remarkably laconic: "I have read your letter carefully. I have taken it to heart. I cannot say any more."

I am not certain whether this is the form letter characteristically sent to critical relatives of patients in mental hospitals. But somehow the complete appropriateness of the reply bespeaks, at least to me, something in suicide that is genuinely arousing of something in us that is deeply intertwined with our very existence.

My second embarrassment has to do with the pretension that I am a scientist. For I find that in order to discuss suicide in a way that appears minimally intelligent to myself I have to introduce the notion of "will," a notion that constitutes an intrinsic challenge to the scientific posture as it is ordinarily recognized. The fundamental polarity out of which science emerges is that between will and necessity, with science specifically declaring for the latter. We have, in science, characteristically sought to find ways of comprehending phenomena in ways that would not call for positing will as a factor. Indeed, in the field of psychology in particular, will has historically been one of the earmarks of approaches that we tend to categorize as unscientific.

However, following the lead which has been given to us by Leslie Farber in his recent book *The Ways of the Will*[1] —a book in which will is recognized as a significant psychological category if not an ontological position—I will allow myself to use the notion. I am covering my embarrassment by hiding behind him in some respect. The fact of the matter is that when we concern ourselves with will we are concerning ourselves with the intrinsic nature of the human being in a way more profound than any enumeration of interacting parameters. It is in the phenomenological nature of the willed act that it should be somewhat incomprehensible. But the ultimate is always intrinsically incomprehensible. The fact is that will arises out of the intrinsic nature of the individual. No matter what variables that act may be conceived as being a function of, if the act is of the will, it is of the intrinsic being of the individual as well. The will is what one is, deeply and to oneself. It is what one is, authentically and really. And its only real necessity is that it is the necessary expression of what the person really is.

But let me not admit too quickly that I must perforce take an unscientific posture. The aim of any science is to learn the truth about its subject matter. And thus, if will seems to be important to understand the nature of suicide, then let us use the notion of will. If it helps us to learn the truth about the nature of the subject matter, its credential is established.

And that is exactly what suicide is: an act of will; an act of will in which the person wills his own death and succeeds in getting his own way. My two embarrassments are really quite relevant. The one pertains to something in us in the contemplation of suicide; the other, to the will. Let us see where this may lead us.

The great modern period of exploring the nature of the human mind was greatly facilitated by the introduction of what was in a certain sense an outrageous contradiction of terms, namely the unconscious wish or the unconscious will, a notion given to us primarily by Freud. The observation that odious wishes go into hiding is extremely valuable not only as an observation in its own right, but also as an aid in making the very study of psychology largely possible. The reason for this is that a wish that is presumed to be unconscious is thereby less odious, precisely because it is not in the region of the will as the will is ordinarily thought of. Thus, for example,

On the Nature of Suicide

I might be attempting to explain the Freudian notion of the Oedipus complex to a novice student. At some point in the dialogue one characteristically arrives at that moment where the student will say something like, "But it's unconscious, though." To which one answers, "Yes, that's right." And it is at that point that the student responds by relaxing and smiling, quite prepared to entertain the notion seriously. Conceiving of the mechanism as unconscious provides a license to entertain it consciously. For if it were a wish conceived of as conscious, odious as it is, it would again have to be driven into unconsciousness.

When we come to suicide, to talk of an unconscious wish to bring about one's own death is often to strain matters. Suicide is characteristically what lawyers refer to as *res ipsa loquitur*—the thing speaks for itself. Certainly the person who has committed suicide is mute and cannot be queried about his intentions. Yet the thing speaks for itself quite clearly, and we hardly need his interpretations. Somehow, the use of the notion of the unconscious wish in its function as a defense mechanism for students of the human psyche is not quite so readily available. Hence, some of our embarrassment.

I might point out parenthetically that the one place where Freud aroused resistance among even his closest associates and most ardent followers was in connection with his notion of the death instinct. Even the defense that the death instinct was unconscious was inadequate to make the full and free entertainment of the notion possible.

Let me now go on with the discussion of the will. Will is the very material out of which guilt is fashioned. In our culture, and perhaps in all cultures, the meting out of punishment is based on evidence that will was involved in the act to be punished. It has been suggested that one of the major ways by which psychoanalysis functions to effect cure is by its ideology which reduced the ontological status of will.

124

Such critics of psychoanalysis as Mowrer have been extremely sensitive to this point in psychoanalysis. But the larger point for our purposes is to see that it is in will that we have one of the most significant loci for psychological distress.

When will is brought to bear on the matter of existence itself, then is it most provocative. It is precisely at the point where will is exerted in connection with existence that the greatest negative reaction is aroused; and this is clearly reflected in the things which have been found odious in the Judeo-Christian tradition. The arrogation of existence to will is the essence of sin for a good deal of the tradition, especially in medieval Catholicism. We observe this in the odiousness associated with the control of birth, making the birth of the child subject to the will; the odiousness of murder, in which one, at will, terminates the life of another; the odiousness of abortion or any willful decision between the life of the mother and the life of the child even in cases where the mother's life is clearly in danger. Some of the Church fathers found that the major sin of Satan was for him to have maintained that he had willed himself into existence. And finally, we note the odiousness of suicide on the part of the historical Catholic Church.

In some important ways the Judeo-Christian tradition manifests great profundity with respect to psychological mechanisms. This is evident in its cognizing a wish for immortality, a wish which, unfortunately, contemporary psychology has been rather sluggish in recognizing. The Biblical story of Adam and Eve in the Garden of Eden is particularly telling. According to the story there are *two* trees in the Garden of Eden, with mankind having partaken of only one of the two. For mankind's sin in having eaten from the one tree punishments are meted out, and they are quite specifically indicated as pain in childbirth and subjection to the dominion of men for women, and hard labor for men. (Our language has rather magnificently equalized the sexes by referring to the pain of childbirth as "labor" pain, which is what happened to Adam.) But the eviction from the Garden of Eden is not so much a punishment—although this interpretation has been given often —but is rather specifically instrumental with respect to the *second* tree. The banishment is specifically to prevent man from eating "of the tree of life" whereby he would then "live forever." Lusting after the tree of life constitutes the real sin of the Judeo-Christian tradition, with at least the Catholic tradition having promised its possibility through the intervention of Jesus Christ. Indeed, the manner in which the Catholic Church has found any other way of winning immortality odious may be interpreted in part as a reaction to competing forms.

Basically, there are two major points in life which should be beyond will: birth and death, the two critical existential moments in a lifetime. The arrogation of will to these two points is found odious.

Within the secular context, the opposite pole from will is necessity. In the religious context, the opposite pole from will is faith. Faith and necessity have the negation of will in common. And, at least in this sense, science is modern man's religion.

The bearing of these considerations on the matter of the suicide is that suicide is clearly an instance of the will being brought to bear on existence.

A few things about the evident place of the will in connection with suicide: Consider a discrepancy that prevails in the literature on suicide, and I have chosen the discrepancy as it appears in various ways. I have chosen between Durkheim and the observations on suicide by Shneidman and Farberow. In spite of the fact that Durkheim was intent upon finding the necessity in suicide, necessity as contrasted with will, he nonetheless defined suicide as a willed act; this is his definition: "The term *suicide* is applied to all cases of death resulting directly or indirectly from a positive or negative act of the victim himself, which he knows will produce this result" (in his *Suicide*).[2] So we have will as part of the definition of suicide in Durkheim. At the same time Shneidman and Farberow, in their book *Clues to Suicide*,[3] in the chapter entitled "The Logic of Suicide," have provided cogent evidence and arguments to the effect that the person who commits suicide is not, in a certain sense, really doing that psychologically. They have suggested that the person who commits suicide has made a *logical* error; that he is one who "cannot successfully imagine his own death and his own complete cessation," who is possessed of "unrealistic feelings of omnipotence and omnipresence," and who thus blunders into death, as though death is some kind of mistake apart from suicide.

In the Durkheim definition of suicide the act would not even be considered to be suicide unless there is evidence that the person clearly knew that he is going to die from his willed act. For Shneidman and Farberow it is basically a mistake as though dying were not quite what was intended, the thought that led to the act being based on "erroneous premises and invalid conclusions" that lead to a "tragic deductive leap into oblivion." In Shneidman and Farberow's view he is not quite willing his own death because, at the very least, he cannot quite imagine what that could be.

I would like to suggest that Durkheim, on the one hand, and Shneidman and Farberow, on the other, are both correct; and that the resolution of the paradox inheres precisely in the fact that in the act of suicide there is the arrogation of the will upon existence; and that *the arrogation of the will upon existence is an important step in a logic which would lead to the conclusion that one might live forever if one only chose to.* The logic is not wrong; it is rather that only half of the empirical proof is forthcoming. To put it most simply: By making one's own death a willed thing, one leaves open the other possibility, that if one did not commit cuicide one would have lived *forever*. By clearly demonstrating that death is under the control of the will it suggests the possibility that life is too; and that if one were to choose not to commit suicide, one would never die. There is at least part-proof that one might live forever if one so willed it.

The paradox between the Durkheim definition and the Shneidman-Farberow observation needs one additional correction. It is not that the person who commits suicide really believes, as Shneidman and Farberow put it, that he is omnipotent. It is rather that there is some doubt in his mind. The doubt calls for proof. The proof is in the very fact that he can bring about his own death through an act of will. This he demonstrates clearly.

One step further: Why might one feel impelled to put one's existence to the test, to test it for immortality, as it were? The answer must be that persons who are led to commit suicide are persons who experience their very beings as acutely "in question." Thus we might expect that a person suffering from a fatal disease might attempt to commit suicide, as well as a person who experiences severe psychosocial isolation, as Durkheim and others have demonstrated to be related to suicide frequencies. These are two sets of conditions that arouse the sense of "being in question." When that sense is aroused one may act to "call the question."

References

[1] Leslie Farber, *The Ways of the Will* (New York: Basic Books, 1966).

[2] Émile Durkheim, *Suicide* (New York: Free Press, 1951).

[3] Edwin S. Shneidman and Norman L. Farberow (Eds.), *Clues to Suicide* (New York: McGraw-Hill, 1957).

12

Sidney M. Jourard

The Invitation
to Die

~~~~~~~~~~~~~~~~~~~~~~~~~~

It seems that we have made giant strides in our
understanding of man—his experience and his behavior—by
comparing him with something else. Our models of man have
been drawn from nature. Thus, we have looked at man as
being like a rat, monkey, pigeon, or guinea-pig; we have assumed that factors that affect the condition of these animals
likewise affect man, the observer of those animals. It is as if
the sciences of human beings have espoused the motto, *"Nihil
animalis a me alienum puto."*

On the Nature of Suicide

And we have compared man to man-made mechanisms and systems: to communication networks, servo-systems, computers, hydraulic systems, robots, and the like, with considerable payoff in understanding the being of man. It is as if we have sought to grasp man by understanding something he has made: *"Nihil machinae a me alienum puto."*

These approaches are embodied in the great efforts to comprehend man: Darwinism, Marxism, psychoanalysis, behaviorism, and physiology.

But there is another approach which I think has become timely, one that science prided itself in surpassing, but which I think can illumine man and the world more than it did hitherto: the approach of animism, or animalism, with the tendency to attribute human motives to the nonhuman beings in the world—a more sophisticated anthropomorphism. From this vantage point, the beings in the world are likened to me as free, conscious agents, with intentionality, and with a career that commences out of nothingness and returns to nothingness. The Latin motto would be something like, *"Nihil mihi a mundi alienum puto"*—"Nothing of my experience can be irrelevant to understanding the world."

The current term for the renascent anthropomorphism, for the use of my experience, as I reflect upon it as a model for the comprehension of the world—and especially the comprehension of the other man in sickness and health, in self-fulfillment and self-destruction—is existential phenomenology. The effort to develop this as a disciplined way of inquiry, a science of persons, is a task of the emerging humanistic psychology.

I address the theme of suicide from the point of view of existential phenomenology.

From this standpoint, man is seen as this particular person, an embodied consciousness, free in a situation of time, place, society, and culture, living a body of specifiable (by others) structure and capabilities, and living in relation to particular other persons. His experience affects and is affected by the disclosed experience of others.

As a person, man is a center for orientation of the entire universe, a perspective through which being is refracted and experienced in a unique way. And man is an origin for action, action which impacts and changes the world (for him and for others), and it changes his own embodied being as well.[1]

A person, so conceived, is not a determined creature, although he encounters determiners as he pursues the fulfillment of his projects in time. Each project, momentary or enduring, to which he has committed himself discloses the world to him in a different way. Thus, a man's biology, anatomy, and physiology may be experienced by him as an obstacle to the fulfillment of some projects, as a facilitator of others. An obese body may handicap the running of a race, but may facilitate the project of pinning an adversary in a wrestling match.

The consciousness which a person is, or embodies, can be likened to an apparatus which receives the disclosures of being, albeit in a highly selective way. We are attentive to some disclosures of being, and inattentive to others, depending upon the projects which animate and direct our lives. And this consciousness of being occurs in numerous modes, sometimes serially, more often fused into an integrated fabric with perceptual, conceptual, imaginative, recollective, affective, and fantasy strands. My experience of you can be analyzed into perceptual, imaginative, conceptual, recollective, and fantasy components. Our experience of anything lends itself to investigation and reporting to another person through the act of reflection, a skill that can be learned.

So much for a sketchy overview of man, seen from the vantage point of existential phenomenology.[2]

On the Nature of Suicide

To live as a person can be likened to amoeboid loco-motion, but locomotion through time, rather than space. Man invents his future being—he imagines himself at some point in the future, whether fifteen seconds or five years ahead; this is one way to describe a project—as an imaginative experience of an as yet unlived way to be in the world. Active life then consists in transmuting the image into a reality that can be perceived by the self, and by others. In this way, life resembles the activity of the artist who transmutes an imaginative ex-perience of his canvas or lump of clay into something that can be perceived. Activity extended in time is necessary for the transmutation. Man pulls himself into the future that he (or someone else) invents for him; he is not pushed by instincts or habit, nor pulled by environmental stimuli. However, a man can repress his experience of freedom or never be awakened to it, and experience himself as driven or controlled by habit, impulse, personal threats, suggestions or invitations from others.

If human life is the *experience* of life, then we can propose that he who experiences more, with greater intensity, lives more. If life occurs in time, then he who has more time has more life.

A person lives as long as he experiences his life as having meaning and value, and as long as he has something to live *for*—meaningful projects that will animate him and invite him into the future or entice him to pull himself into the future. He will continue to live as long as he has hope of fulfilling meanings and values. As soon as meaning, value, and hope vanish from a person's experience, he begins to stop living; that is, he begins to die.

I am going to propose that people destroy themselves in response to an invitation originating from others that he stop living. And that people live in response to the experience

132

of chronic invitations to continue living in some way or in any possible way. Life and death can be seen fruitfully as responses to an invitation or the experience of an invitation. The invitation is extended by others, that is, it originates in someone's consciousness, sometimes as a conscious wish that the person stop existing, in that way, or at all, sometimes as an unconscious wish; sometimes not so openly, but rather as an indifference to the continued existence of the person in question. In whatever mode the wish for death, or the indifference to continued existence, appears, it is communicated to the one whom we might call the suicide. He experiences himself as being invited to stop living, and he obliges. (Actually, he may only be invited to stop that way of living.) He may accept the invitation by shooting himself, taking sleeping pills, jumping off a bridge, or jumping into the path of a car; or he may commit suicide more slowly by stopping his projects, disintegrating himself such that he is ostensibly killed by germs and viruses that have killed him because his immunity mechanisms have been called out of action; or he commits suicide by suspending or diminishing his vigilance toward all the things that are always present to kill a person, but which ordinarily he averts or neutralizes when he experiences his existence as having value, when he has things to do, and projects to fulfill.

I am going to postulate that there are in our bodies some self-destruct mechanisms that are always present.[3] And in the environment there are agencies that can release these self-destruct mechanisms. Physicians have catalogued all the germs, bacteria, and viruses that can become self-destruct agencies. I am proposing that we have enough inside us to kill an army, but that usually these are held in abeyance as long as the person experiences his life as meaningful and hopeful and valuable. Anything that diminishes a person's experience of hope, meaning, and value to his continued existence has simply released the activity of the self-destruct mechanisms faster than they would have been released by ordinary wear and tear.

I postulate that official views of life expectancy to which a person has been trained provide one source of accelerated self-destruction. Thus, many cultures have no role for more than a few people past a certain age; nor have they the food or shelter for more than a limited number of members of their tribe and group. And so when a person has reached the age at which he is expected to die, if he has been effectively socialized into the world-view of that culture, he obliges by dying. He is assisted in this project by the expectations of others that he will not be around for long. In fact, he may have become a dead being in the consciousness of others before he has died. (The parallel with voodoo death is obvious.) If there is any empirical validity to this analysis—and average death ages in various societies lend at least some credence to it —then it becomes meaningful to redefine "natural death from old age" as at once murder and suicide—an invitation to die, extended by others, that has been accepted by the victim.

People who have not been fully socialized and mystified may escape the death sentence by not taking seriously traditional or authoritative views as to the proper time to die; or they may take them seriously, but defy the invitations that they experience.[4]

Our society trains people to expect to live to riper ages than it did one hundred years ago. But we kill our citizens in another way—by encouraging them to believe that there is only one identity, one role, one way for them to be, one value for them to fulfill. When this ground for their existence is outgrown or lost, a person may begin to die or he may kill himself more quickly. I have in mind here those instances of people who kill themselves after the loss of money, work, a limb, their beauty, their sexuality, a loved one, or status, and those persons who, on reflection, discover that they no longer are the person they believed themselves to be. And so, by killing themselves, they are saying, in effect, that they believe they have only one incarnation that is possible for them, one way to live and be. When the ground or value of their existence is eliminated, so is their existence. I suspect that our socialization practices encourage people to believe that they can only *be* in one way such that they cannot imagine or invent new purposes, new identities, new lives when an old one has run its course. In fact, I believe that most of what we call mental and physical illness is evidence that the way in which the person had been living up to the point of his collapse has truly been outgrown and it is time for him to stop that way of life to invent a new way which is more compatible with health. But members of our healing and helping professions construe the signals that a way of life has been outlived as an illness to be cured, rather than a call to stop, reflect, meditate, dream, and invent a new self. The helping professions do not so much help a person to live as they help him to perpetuate a life that has been outgrown. I suspect that our ossified theories of disease and health have the sociological function of perpetuating the social, economic and political status quo. People stay vital, growing, fit, and zestful as a function of the way they live their lives. They live their lives for meaningful projects. When projects are outworn, it is time to re-project, not anesthetize the experience of despair, or disinfect the gut; because if the "sick" person resumes the life that was sickening him, it will soon kill him. Can it be that physicians, psychiatrists, psychologists, social workers, and clergymen help society retain its stability, its present class structure and distribution of wealth and freedom by encouraging people not to reinvent themselves when it is time to? Is it suicidal for a person to consult an established practitioner?[5]

When a person feels he cannot live any more in the

way that he has been, when he feels trapped in frozen interpersonal relationships in a social system that he feels offers
him no way out, he may fall physically ill, become schizophrenic or psychotically depressed, or commit murder or suicide. (In fact, to murder someone else is one way to get others,
or the state, to kill you.) But the experience of entrapment is
just that—an experience. Human consciousness being what it
is, it can be mystified and trained in ways that fixate habits
of construing; and it can be liberated such that a person,
feeling trapped by one way of construing his situation, can
untrap himself by an imaginative and creative reconstruing of
the situation. We can ask, how do we typically train people
in the activity of construing and in the activity of imagining?
My view is that, typically, we train people to an impoverished
imagination, to a banal image of their possibilities, and to
conventional ways to attach meaning. We train people to repress their experience of freedom and to replace it with the
conviction that in certain situations they "have no choice."
Our way of socializing is effective at producing a social system
that has an immense productive output and much material
wealth, but at the cost of alienating most of us from the experience of our own possibilities—including the possibility of
reinventing ourselves and reconstruing our situations of felt
entrapment. Any social practices, such as stupefying television
or mystifying mass media, that gain control over people's
consciousness contribute to sickness, madness, and self-destruction just as they contribute to maintenance of the status quo.
Any teacher who liberates, expands, or activates a person's
consciousness creates a condition for richer life of longer duration.

The invitation to die, if given openly—"Why don't
you drop dead"—can be vigorously declined. An invitation
to die given in bad faith, as a fantasy wish that is communicated subvocally or that is conveyed as indifference, is more

subtle and thus more difficult for a person to counter. I suspect that, just as Laing and Esterson were able to document the way family members of schizophrenic girls communicated their wish that the victim annihilate her own perspective and replace it with one that was alien, then denied it all,[6] so we might find, for people who kill themselves or who die before they "should," evidence of the wish that they die existing at some level of consciousness in the people around them. Or else we would find that the more speedily dying person experiences himself as not existing for others.

The implications that I see in this analysis are to the effect that it is possible to study a social system or an interpersonal nexus in order to see in what ways the invitations to die are communicated, to discover where they originate, and to explore ways to counter them. And it is possible to study socialization practices, medical and healing ideologies and practices, to ascertain in what ways they fail to activate a person's experience of his freedom, his creative imagination, and his freedom to reinvent himself, when one way of being has palpably become unlivable any longer. Surely there are other alternatives to entrapment than physical illness, psychosis, or suicide. I think we need, in our society, to take the precept, "Ye must be born again" out of Sunday School and put it into our public schools. I think we need to liberalize and pluralize our social structure, so that people can be taught a theory of personal growth that encourages them to let *an* incarnation die, without killing their embodied selves so that they can invent new ones, and find places and company to live them, until they die of being worn out. Meditation and retreat centers, rather than hospitals, where the invitation to live is seriously extended; and where guides are available to help a person kill off the identity he has outgrown (not his body) so he can invent a new one—these may be an answer to the problem of self-destruction. And if we make our society even more pluralistic, people can take a perspective that is unlivable in one scene to another where it is welcomed; or be encouraged to return to their old scenes, but in a reincarnated way. We need to learn how to invite people to explore and try more of their possibilities than modal upbringing seems to foster so that the invitation to live and grow is as fascinating as is the invitation to die.[7]

One mark of a good theory, as of an enlightened and growing perspective, is its power to reconcile contradiction.[8] A good theory of suicide should make both living-behavior and dying-behavior intelligible. I think that Bakan's recent book[9] contains the ingredients of such a theory, one which students of suicide might well examine carefully. Earlier (1959, 1960, 1961) I offered some rather crude speculations that I regard as less documented versions of Bakan's later and more sophisticated concepts. I spoke of "inspiritation," "spirit-titre," and "dispiritation," all terms that refer to the extent to which a person is integrated. When a person is inspirited, according to these views, his body is maximally organized or integrated such that behavior is frictionless (muscles and endocrine and neural systems are synergic), and subjectively, the person is characterized by good morale, enthusiasm, a sense of meaning, direction, and purpose in his existence. Events, relationships, and situations can dispirit a person, such that the entire system that a man is becomes less resistant to infectious diseases and entropic forces. Thus, according to this view, for one person to disconfirm another, to reduce his hope, or to diminish the value he invests in his aims and purposes is to accelerate his rate of dying. To inspirit a person is to augment and confirm his values and purposes, to increase his experience of meaning in his existence, and to render him more resistant both to physical and mental diseases.[10]

Bakan has introduced the concept of "deferential"

dying—wherein an organism does to itself what it anticipates and believes the environment is going to do to it—and the concept of "telic decentralization." The latter term refers, in humans, to a relinquishing of the purposes that give direction and meaning to a person's life (at the phenomenological level) and isomorphically permit the organization of subordinate processes to operate unchecked by the higher *telos*—a factor in cancer and other physical diseases. Bakan adduces a great deal of empirical evidence to buttress his thesis, and to me it makes a great deal of sense. Moreover, both his theory and mine have many practical implications. If a person carries within him the means whereby his body can destroy itself and if the environment carries myriad means for destroying a person, the problem to be explained is not suicide or death, but rather, living in the face of so many physical pathogens and so many experiences of invitation to abandon life.

One person can invite another to change his being in many ways. I can invite you to change the meanings you attach to things and events to reconstrue your world.[11] I can invite you to change from the inauthentic way to the authentic way.[12] It follows that I can invite you to try living again when you have experienced yourself as invited to die, when your purposes have worn out, when it seems that there is no place for you and your way of being a person in a given time and place, and when you feel you have already been abandoned by others. I can invite you to reinvent yourself, your purposes, and you might become reinspirited, characterized by renewed telic centralization.

Disintegration, telic decentralization, is posited by Bakan as both a condition of self-destruction and a condition for growth, for further differentiation of an organism or a person. I believe that growth is characterized as a kind of dying (the end of the tether, the end of projects, giving up, becoming psychotic to some degree) followed by a rebirth—of new challenges and fascinations and invitations. These formulations adumbrate nicely with Bakan's. The suicide, especially the younger suicide, may be seen as one who has reached the end of his tether, of his projects, and he will, unless effectively invited to live, erroneously believe that he cannot live further, and so he kills himself. Let us, then, as therapists and healers, inquire into the phenomenon of invitation, since it appears to affect physiology, experience, and behavior.

References

[1] See R. D. Laing, *The Politics of Experience* (New York: Pantheon, 1967) for a more detailed formulation of a person from the viewpoint of existential phenomenology.

[2] Further development of these ideas is given in S. M. Jourard, *Disclosing Man to Himself* (Princeton: Van Nostrand, 1968).

[3] Bakan has proposed a mechanism which he calls "telic decentralization," which goes a long way toward making this phenomenon intelligible. See D. Bakan, *Disease, Pain and Sacrifice: Toward a Psychology of Suffering* (Chicago: University of Chicago Press, 1968).

[4] It occurs to me that one approach to the problem of aging people who do not wish to die of boredom, nor yet to add to the problem of overpopulation, is to create an agency, like an employment agency, specifically for people in their sixties and older, with international connections. Men and women who have been obliged to retire, and who might then age and die rapidly, could be given the opportunity to "export" themselves to other places, other countries even, where their knowledge and competence would be welcomed, rather than be assessed as obsolete. We already export obsolete munitions, automobiles, buses, and machinery to developing countries.

[5] See T. Szasz, *The Myth of Mental Illness* (New York: Hoeber, 1961).

[6] Cf. R. D. Laing, *Self and Others* (London: Tavistock, 1961)

140

and R. D. Laing and A. Esterson, *Sanity, Madness and the Family* (London: Tavistock, 1964).

[7] A psychotherapeutic implication that I see here is the following: If research can show that some regimen, some profession, some role carries with it a high probability of developing serious illness, and a low mean age for dying, then an unenlightened person living in that way is speeding up his dying. A therapist's job would be to let him know these facts, so that if he continues living in that way, it is tantamount to suicide. Of course the patient could choose that path if he wished. An intense but brief life is, for many persons, preferable to a long, safe, and boring existence.

[8] Cf. Franklin J. Shaw, *Reconciliation, a Theory of Man Transcending,* edited by S. M. Jourard and D. C. Overlade (Princeton: Van Nostrand, 1966).

[9] Bakan, *op. cit.*

[10] S. M. Jourard, *The Transparent Self* (Princeton: Van Nostrand, 1964).

[11] Cf. G. A. Kelly, *The Psychology of Personal Constructs* (New York: Norton, 1955).

[12] Cf. Jourard, *Disclosing Man to Himself.*

Index

Index

144

Index

M

MENNINGER, K., 13, 18, 35, 41n, 91
METCHNIKOFF, E., 36, 42n
Mortality, as philosophical question: animism, 129–131; Buber, 104–106, 110n; Choron, 33–42; Dostoyevsky, 103–104, 110n; existential phenomenology, 129–141; Heidegger, 120; and immortality, 120–128; William James, 41; Kierkegaard, 106–107; Nietzsche, 104, 110n; St. Augustine, 35; Sartre, 41; Schopenhauer, 36–39; Toynbee, 23–24; de Unamuno, 121
MURRAY, H. A., 28, 69

N

NASH definitions of death, 18
National Institute of Mental Health, 45–46; Center for Studies of Suicide Prevention, 7
NIETZSCHE, F., 104, 110n

O

OPPENHEIM, D. E., 4, 18, 60–61, 63, 67n, 76

P

Philosophers on suicide (*see* Mortality)

Prevention of suicide (*see* Suicide prevention)
Psychoanalysis and suicide, 51, 76–77, 114, 116, 123–124
Psychodynamics of suicide, 8–17, 22–28, 115–118

R

Research on suicide, 24–28, 55–63; need for, 89–90; statistical problems, 95–99

S

St. Augustine, 35
SARTRE, J. P., 41
SCHOPENHAUER, A., 36–39, 42n
SHNEIDMAN, E. S., 13, 30n, 67n, 69, 73n, 79, 117, 119n, 126–128
Statistics on suicide, 24–28, 95–99
STEKEL, W., 2, 8–9, 59, 67n
Student suicide, 49–50, 53–67, 76
Suicide: and age, 10–18; and Christian tradition, 125–126; definitions of, 112, 114, 119n; and education, 3, 49–50, 53–67, 76; effect on others, 20–26, 77–78, 87–88; and environment, 3, 6–7, 53–67; prevention of, 5, 7–8, 19–22, 43–47, 93–95; psychoanalytic approach to, 51, 76–77, 114, 116, 123–124; psychodynamics of, 8–17, 22–28, 115–118; research and statistics, 24–28, 55–63, 89–99; romanticization of, 28, 68–70; and Will, 4, 35–39,

Index

40n–41n, 103–128 (*see also* Death; Mortality; *and specific headings, as* Will, Research)

Suicide prevention, intervention, and postvention, 5, 7–8, 19–22, 43–47; in England, 44, 93–95; financing, 46–47; lay volunteers, 45–46, 93–95; in U.S., 7, 8, 45

Suicidology: American Association of Suicidology, 1, 4, 8, 18–19, 29n, 30n; historical interest, 49–51; modern scope, 6–30

T

TABACHNICK, N. D., 35, 42n

Todestrieb (*see* Death drive)

TOYNBEE, A., 16, 23–28, 30n

U

UNAMUNO, M. DE, 121

V

Vienna psychoanalytic symposium, 1910: as blueprint for research, 49–52; and education, 53–67; historical descriptions of, 2–3, 17–18, 29n, 49, 53–55, 74–76

W

WAHL, C., 34, 41n

WALD, G., 7, 30n

WEISMAN, A. D., 11, 30n

WESTCOTT, W. W., 50, 52n

Will: and Judeo-Christian tradition, 124–126; and suicide, 4, 35–39, 40n–41n, 103–128

Z

ZILBOORG, G., 76, 80n